BEHOLD THE LEVIATHAN

ADVANCE PRAISE FOR THE BOOK

'Neither standard economic metrics nor stock market valuations can do justice to the remarkable dynamics underpinning India's revival as a country that matters in the global scheme of things. *Behold the Leviathan* captures succinctly the multidimensional nature of both India's progress and its challenges. If you are invested in India, financially or emotionally, you should read this book'—**Ashish Dhawan, founder–chairperson, Central Square Foundation and founder–trustee, Ashoka University**

'To successfully invest in India, it is important to understand the nature of economic and social change in this vast country. *Behold the Leviathan* is therefore an essential read for anyone who is putting money to work in this rapidly growing economy'—**Harsh Mariwala, chairman, Marico Ltd**

'*Behold the Leviathan* sheds light on hitherto unexplored aspects of India's remarkable ascent. To get a thorough understanding of modern India, with all its twists and turns, you must read this book!'—**Nandan Nilekani, chairman and co-founder, Infosys and founding chairman, UIDAI (Aadhaar)**

'The economic transformation of a complex country such as India can never be told as a linear narrative. *Behold the Leviathan* does a wonderful job of analysing the different dimensions along which India is changing. I found the book to be a riveting read'—**Niranjan Rajadhyaksha, executive director, Artha Global**

'*Behold the Leviathan* is that rare compelling read on the Indian economy which you can read for pleasure or for profit. It explains in clear terms the economic success underway in India today and highlights several fascinating subplots within the master narrative'—**Pirojsha Adi Godrej, executive chairman, Godrej Properties**

'*Behold the Leviathan* skilfully maps out just how dramatically conditions in India have changed over the past two decades in favour of enterprising small business owners'—**Sanjeev Bikhchandani, founder and executive vice chairman, Info Edge (India) Ltd**

'*Behold the Leviathan: The Unusual Rise of Modern India* is a groundbreaking exploration of India's rapid economic and social transformation over the past decade. This compelling book will challenge decision-makers, policymakers and opinion leaders to re-evaluate their long-standing perceptions of India's development. It provides a profound understanding of the country's unexpected ascendancy and social progress, making it an essential read for anyone seeking to grasp the true dynamics of modern India'—**T.V. Mohandas Pai, chairman, 3one4 Capital**

'Going beyond the quotidian matters which tend to characterize daily economic discourse in India, *Behold the Leviathan* explores India's evolution through the lens of social and commercial change. The result is a firecracker of a book packed with interesting analyses and striking conclusions'—**Vellayan Subbiah, executive vice chairman, Tube Investments of India and chairman, Cholamandalam (Chola) Investment and Finance Co. Ltd**

BEHOLD THE LEVIATHAN

The Unusual Rise of Modern India

SAURABH MUKHERJEA
AND NANDITA RAJHANSA

PENGUIN
BUSINESS

An imprint of Penguin Random House

PENGUIN BUSINESS

Penguin Business is an imprint of the Penguin Random House group of companies
whose addresses can be found at global.penguinrandomhouse.com

Published by Penguin Random House India Pvt. Ltd
4th Floor, Capital Tower 1, MG Road,
Gurugram 122 002, Haryana, India

First published in Penguin Business by Penguin Random House India 2024

10 9 8 7 6 5 4 3

The views and opinions expressed in this book are the authors' own and the
facts are as reported by them, which have been verified to the extent possible,
and the publishers are not in any way liable for the same.

Please note that no part of this book may be used or reproduced in any manner for the
purpose of training artificial intelligence technologies or systems.

ISBN 9780143469490

Typeset in Adobe Caslon Pro by MAP Systems, Bengaluru, India
Printed at Replika Press Pvt. Ltd, India

www.penguin.co.in

For those who toil so that India can rise

Contents

x   Contents

Preface

Both of us studied economics at a postgraduate level. As we were doing so, we came across a body of literature on the Indian economy that either sees India as a broken economy or as a shining exemplar, a country on the ascent. Such polarized accounts of the economy we do not believe do justice to the multifaceted nature of change playing out in twenty-first-century India. To be specific, there are three different dimensions of change that we believe are neglected in the popular discourse on the Indian economy:

- **Two steps forward, one step back:** No free-market democracy moves forward in a linear fashion. Periods of growth are typically followed by periods of economic hardship. Part of this is due to the nature of the economic cycle wherein periods of economic expansion typically result in inflation rising, as sooner or later demand outstrips supply. Rising inflation is then countered by policymakers through hikes in interest rates that then slow down the economy. If these rate hikes continue for an extended period of time and/or are accompanied by other shocks to the economy e.g. rising oil prices, then the economy often enters a period of low or negative economic growth.

  However, distinct from the economic cycle, the other reason free-market democracies go forward two steps and then go back a step is because vested interests step in to arrest the advancement of the economy if things are not playing out in their favour. So, for example, Japan's unprecedented burst of economic growth in the forty years following the end of World War II was brought to an end by the Plaza Accord of 1985 which signalled the beginning of an extended period of the yen appreciating relative to the US dollar (46 per cent appreciation in real effective terms by the end of 1986 itself).[1] American manufacturers had prevailed upon the Republican government to engineer this intervention that helped arrest the rise of highly efficient Japanese companies like Toyota, Honda, Sony and Panasonic. The sustained appreciation of the yen in the face of American coercion ultimately pushed Japan into a thirty-year period of economic stagnation. However, just because Japan's economic progress was arrested after four decades of progress does not negate the fact that those four decades transformed Japan from a country devastated by World War II to one of the most prosperous societies in the world.

Similarly, the ongoing bull run in the Indian stock market is now entering its fifth year with the BSE500 having more than tripled from its April 2002 low of 10,527. More than 120 million new retail investors have entered the Indian stock market because of its 33 per cent annualized returns over more than four years. Given that only 80 million people file personal Income Tax returns in India, it is all but certain that many of the newcomers to the Indian stock market are low-income earners who are likely to see much of their life's savings wiped out in the correction that tends to follow such breathless rallies. However, that correction—and its attendant downsides—do NOT negate the unequivocal benefits that accrue to the Indian economy from a rising stock market e.g. the drop in the cost of equity capital and the shift in household savings from unproductive physical assets to more productive financial assets. Understanding the uneven nature of economic progress is essential for those who aspire to emerge from economic and financial cycles, stronger rather than weaker.

- **Winners and losers:** Not only do free-market democracies create winners and losers but the winners tend to be few, and their margin of victory tends to be huge. In contrast, the losers are numerous, and their losses tend to look enormous in comparison to the spoils that accrue to the winners. This, rather than being a bug, is a design feature of capitalism.[2] The force behind this design feature is the Power Law, which posits that in any competitive economic situation (e.g. the stock market or a high-stakes sports tournament such as the Wimbledon), a very high proportion of the gains will accrue to a small minority of participants (e.g. the Wimbledon champion's prize money is 50x that of the player who loses in the first round).[3]
  The nature of economic progress therefore creates inequality and India is no stranger to such an inequitable distribution of spoils. Understanding these inequalities helps not just investors but also other decision-makers such as CEOs and policymakers make better decisions.

- **Interplay of Social and Economic Change:** Literature on the Indian economy that discusses issues such as unemployment, income inequality and budget deficits without reference to the rich interplay between society and the economy is incomplete at best and misleading at worst. Although India is the world's fifth-largest economy, it is only the 136th richest country in the world when ranked on its per capita income of around

Rs 2.4 lakh or $2,700. When such a country, ranked amongst the sixty poorest nations in the world, makes a transition from grinding poverty to second world status, it is but natural social and economic change will go hand in hand. As the economic historian Joel Mokyr describes in his outstanding book on the origins of the knowledge economy, *The Gifts of Athena* (2004), the industrial revolution and the subsequent multi-century growth surge of the West owed much to the rise of social networks comprising universities, publishers, scientists, guilds, trade bodies and kindred institutions. Through these networks, knowledge was generated and disseminated and that in turn drove technological change and economic growth. The networking of India is driving a similar cycle of ideation, innovation and growth in the most unexpected corners of Indian society. One of the privileges of living and working in India today is to witness these networks and these cycles in full operational flow on a daily basis.

In this book, we have tried to bring alive these three dimensions of change in the Indian economy. We hope *Behold the Leviathan: The Unusual Rise of Modern India* will help you make informed judgement calls regarding India. We would like to hear from you and learn from your perspectives on India. If you are willing to share them, then leviathan@marcellus.in is the email address via which you can contact us.

Nandita Rajhansa and Saurabh Mukherjea
Mumbai, July 2024

(Disclaimer: The authors, their families, Marcellus Investment Managers and the firm's clients may have a beneficial interest in the companies mentioned in this book. The material in this book is neither investment research, nor investment advice.)

Prologue

From Konappana Agrahara to Electronic City: A Village as a Microcosm of India

> We are much better off dreaming, taking risks and trying to realize a billion aspirations; at best we risk falling flat on our faces. Far more egregious, and most dangerous to our country, is going about 'business as usual', leaving a billion voices unheard and a billion frustrations unresolved.
>
> —Nandan Nilekani, chairman of Infosys, in *Rebooting India: Realizing a Billion Aspirations* (2015)

Exhibit 1: Electronics City—then (1990s) and now (2020s)[1]

Source: Reddit, *Deccan Herald*; images used only for illustration purposes, their copyrights remain with their respective creators

Introduction

It was a typical summer in 1991 in Konappana Agrahara and Doddathogur, two villages located 20 km from the centre of

Bangalore city. The farmers here were busy sowing paddy and ragi, waiting for the upcoming monsoon, which usually hits Karnataka by June. The monsoon arrived on time and filled the many reservoirs and lakes around these villages. That year, along with monsoon also came the economic reforms that opened up the Indian economy and marked a major upshift in the country's economic fortunes. In the summer of 1991, unaware of just how dramatically these reforms would change their lives over the next few years, the farmers in Konappana Agrahara and Doddathogur continued with the backbreaking effort that goes into the tilling of the earth.

In 1991, a square foot of land in these villages cost Rs 23; and land in the city centres of Bangalore (now Bengaluru) and Bombay (now Mumbai) cost Rs 3600 and Rs 16,000, respectively.[2] Fast-forward to 2023 . . . a square foot of land in Electronic City (as the area around the two villages is known today) costs between Rs 5000 and Rs 6000. That implies a compound aggregate growth rate of approximately 20 per cent over thirty-two years. This period has seen these agrarian villages transform into urban landscapes dotted with multi-lane, multi-level highways and multi-storeyed residential and commercial buildings.

Exhibit 2: The landscape of Bengaluru and Electronics City in the 2020s[3]

Source: Google Maps, Bing images; the images here are only for illustration purposes, their copyrights remain with their respective creators

How did Konappana Agrahara and Doddathogur become Electronic City, home to the gleaming headquarters of prominent Indian firms like Infosys, Titan and Happiest Minds? There are broadly three phases in this story of transformation.

Phase 1: Foundation of Electronics City in 1978

In the 1970s, while the ragi and paddy farmers in these villages went about their business, one man was nursing a vision to make Bangalore the next Silicon Valley. This man was Ram Krishna Baliga, chairman of Karnataka State Electronics Development Corporation (Keonics). In 1978, he established Electronics City on 332 acres of land from Konappana Agrahara and Doddathogur villages. Gradually, through the 1980s, this area became home to several electronics-related manufacturing industries. However, it wasn't until the liberalization of 1991 that development in this area truly picked up pace.

Phase 2: The Reforms of 1991 and the Entry of IT Services in India

In the summer of 1991, then prime minister P.V. Narasimha Rao and his finance minister, Dr Manmohan Singh, opened up the Indian economy to the world at large. These economic reforms breathed new life into the nascent IT services industry in India.

Established in 1981, Infosys went public in 1992. As its business grew by leaps and bounds, it needed a larger office space, for which purpose it purchased a large parcel of land, roughly the area of one and a half football fields, from Keonics in Electronics City. This is where Infosys's first campus came up, in 1993 (see the picture below, of the colossal current-day Infosys campus in Electronic City). N.R. Narayana Murthy is quoted as saying in his 2018 biography authored by Ritu Singh:

Having acquired land from the state of Karnataka in Bengaluru, the company built a 160,000 square feet campus on five acres in a Software Technology Park in Electronics City and made it its headquarters. This prism-shaped structure is not merely a striking piece of architecture in the city, its inhabitants and corporate culture are of a standard and nature that has caught the attention of the world.

This move by Infosys into Electronics City served as an inflection point for the area. After that, development here went into hyper-drive. More companies started setting up their offices and campuses here. With these offices came tens of thousands of highly skilled white-collar workers. These workers and their families started settling down in the area around Electronics City.

Exhibit 3: The Infosys Campus in Electronic City Spans 81 Acres (Equivalent to Thirty Football Fields)[4]

Source: Bing images; images used only for illustration purposes, their copyrights remain with their respective creators

Companies preferred this area because Bengaluru, even at that time, had excellent educational institutes like Indian Institute of Management (Bangalore) (IIM-B) and the Indian Institute of Science (IISc). In addition, the longstanding presence of public sector giants—like Hindustan Aeronautics Ltd (HAL), Hindustan Machine Tools (HMT), Bharat Electronics Ltd (BEL), Defence

Research and Development Organization (DRDO) and Indian Space Research Organization (ISRO)—meant that even in the early 1990s, the city had a large talent pool from which the IT services companies could draw their employees.

Just as importantly, the people of this city were largely welcoming of the migrant population that would continue to pour into the city in the decades to come. The residents of these two villages had no aversion to Hindi, and both the northern and southern cultures were effortlessly assimilated into the social fabric of the newly emerging Bengaluru Metropolitan Region.

Phase 3: Electronic City Becomes a Global IT Hub in the Twenty-First Century

As India became the unchallenged IT services hub of the world through the first two decades of the twenty-first century, Electronic City boomed. According to the latest estimates available, Electronic City employs over 100,000 people[5] within its area of 3 square kilometres.

By 1997, the upkeep of Electronics City was transferred from Keonics to Electronics City Industries Association (ELCIA), and the development process gained further traction. ELCIA is an independent apex body serving the interests of all the electronics industries situated in the cluster. It not only represents the interests of all the companies situated in the area, but also provides skill development support and mentorship, and hosts job fairs for the Micro, Small and Medium Enterprises (MSMEs) in the area.

As more tech workers found employment in Electronics City, it drove a growing need for high-quality housing. This in turn led to the commissioning of Phase 2 of Electronics City in the late 1990s. Large residential projects started coming up in and around this area to cater to the demand. In what was once a geography consisting of half a dozen lakes and reservoirs, water became scarcer as offices, apartments, roads and highways got built. To connect this booming tech hub with Bengaluru proper, a new elevated multi-lane road was inaugurated in 2010—the Electronic City Elevated Expressway is a 10-km elevated highway from the infamous (for its traffic jams!) Silk Board junction in Bengaluru city to Electronic City (the right-hand picture in Exhibit 1 shows the expressway).

Exhibit 4: The Shopping Precinct in Electronic City[6]

Source: Marcellus Investment Managers

So, who were the winners and losers as these tranquil villages became a booming tech hub over the course of three decades?

Three Sets of Big Winners

The first set of beneficiaries of Electronic City consists of the Indian IT services firms and the large MNCs who have set up campuses here. They were able to get what is now prime real estate in Bengaluru Metropolitan Region at a bargain basement rate. For example, Infosys acquired a large parcel of land in Electronic City for approximately Rs 40 lakh ($50K) in 1992. Today, the price of the same piece of land (just the land) has risen 240 times, to roughly Rs 100 crores ($12 mn). Infosys is just one of the more than 100[7] major employers in Electronic City (others include HCL Tech, Siemens, TCS, Texas Instruments, Hewlett Packard, Titan and Wipro), almost all of whom have been able to build highly cost-efficient and yet world-class businesses locking into India's skilled, low-cost talent combined with low-cost real estate.

The second set of beneficiaries consists of the people working in these companies. As demand for skills has boomed, the office workers in Electronic City have found many takers for their talents. In fact, if we look at the per capita income of the Bengaluru Urban district (which includes Electronic City), it has crossed Rs 6 lakh per annum[8], three times the national average. Even Mumbai, India's financial capital, has not been able to keep up; per capita income in the city is Rs 3.44 lakh ($4K)[9], half the level of Bengaluru's!

Income aside, the diversity of talent in Electronic City's multi-cultural and multi-ethnic offices has resulted in the creation of a vibrant community of well-educated, globally mobile and highly aspirational professionals.

The third set of beneficiaries consists of the large landowners or landlords in the area. People who still own land in and around Electronic City have become rupee millionaires, courtesy the 240 times escalation in land prices over the last thirty years. Assuming that half of the area in Electronic City (roughly 450 acres out of the ~900 acres[10]; note: 450 acres would be roughly equivalent to 150 football fields) is with the landlords, where on average the rent per month is Rs 3 lakh per acre[11], then each year the rent collection by these landlords would amount to Rs 160 crore ($20mn).

Let's contrast this with the same acreage of land being deployed in agriculture. One harvest of paddy will yield the farmers an in-hand profit of roughly Rs 50,000 per acre,[12] which means a total harvest profit of roughly Rs 2.25 crore per annum (from the 450 acres of cultivable land in Electronic City). Assuming that there are two harvest seasons in a year (paddy will not grow in both seasons and prices will vary, but for simplicity's sake we are using this assumption), the total profit generated per annum will be Rs 4.5 crore ($0.5mn), roughly 3 per cent of what could've been earned had the same land been rented out to the big employers of Electronic City.

Who Has Lost as Electronic City Boomed?

The first set of losers would be the landless labourers who used to work on the farms of Konappana Agrahara and Doddathogur villages. With the farms gone, these labourers would have either had to relocate elsewhere in the interiors of Karnataka to continue to earn a living in rural India or service the incoming migrant population by undertaking taxing day jobs like cleaning, sweeping or cooking for meagre wages, or head towards the factories of Hosur in Tamil Nadu, an industrial belt which is 25 km south-east of Electronic City.

The wages in a factory in Hosur are generally north of Rs 4 lakh per annum[13]. This is significantly more than what a farm labourer in Karnataka would earn today. One could argue that the farm labourers who have found employment in the industrial belts of south India are actually better off for their involuntary dislocation from Electronic City. Unfortunately, the factories of south India employ in total just 6 million[14] workers. So there is a distinct possibility that many of the erstwhile farm labourers of the two villages that became Electronic City are continuing their struggle to earn a living in rural India.

As Electronic City developed, with multiple companies setting up shop and employing affluent white-collar professionals, the associated cost of living in the area also rose rapidly. Rentals, food prices, transport costs, all surged. While the white-collar professionals could afford this as their incomes rose at a much faster pace (thanks to pay hikes and promotions) than the rise in the cost of living, the landless labourers who had no specific skills that gave them bargaining power in the labour market saw their incomes and savings dwindle in real terms i.e., after adjusting for inflation. Today, an annual income of Rs 2.5 lakh ($3000) is enough for a comfortable life in rural south India, but is barely enough to scrape by in an urbanized area like Electronic City.

The Rs 6 lakh ($7000) average per capita income of Bengaluru Metropolitan region is, in this sense, deceptive. According to the 2011 census,[15] there were around 98,000 people classified as agricultural labourers (i.e., workers who do NOT own land) and around 95,000 as cultivators (i.e., farmers who own land), making for around 1 per cent of the total population of the Bengaluru Urban district each. The standard of living of these people is likely to have fallen in a booming suburban district like Electronic City.

The Uncertain Winners

There is a third category of people in Electronic City whose benefit/loss arithmetic isn't as clear-cut as for the previous two categories. These are largely the people involved in the intermediation trade—i.e., the local kirana store owners, grain traders, 3W drivers or small- and medium-enterprise (SME) owners. Their story in the new economic realities of modern India is not as straightforward as it is in the context of a village economy (i.e., a small and sheltered economy) where the competitive intensity is lower and they enjoy better profit margins. This was the case in the pre-1991 era of Electronics City, where small shop owners, auto drivers and small business owners had complete control over the local economy and transportation system in that geography.

With the 'opening up' of the Electronic City economy to external competition (from the wider Bengaluru region), the local monopoly benefits slipped away from these small entrepreneurs with two sets of forces kicking in, at least in the retail space—the entry of organized and efficient players like

D-Mart, and e-commerce platforms like Big Basket. This led to some loss of relevance, more than anything else, for the local kirana stores, as most of the migrant population in the city that did not have strong relationships built with them inevitably started using the organized players' services. Another example of this is the upending of the local auto drivers' lives by the entry of organized transport service providers like Uber and Ola in Electronic City. Even though today the local auto drivers are servicing a higher number of passengers than they used to in the pre-Uber/Ola days, they are not able to generate the same profit per ride they once did.

Having said that, smart business owners and intermediaries have found ways to thrive in a booming urban area like Electronic City. Sumit Ghorawat, founder of ShopKirana, a B2B company that provides technology and supply chain management tools to retailers, says, 'Any ordinary grocery retailer in most areas earns anywhere in the region of 10–15 per cent gross margins on an average. Now, while it may not be as high as that of established and larger chains like D-Mart or Star Bazaar, it's enough for sustenance of the business.'

If, over and above this, small retailers decide to go online and display their inventory to their customers on an app, they may be able to attract customers who are looking for specific products, enabling demand-supply matching. Furthermore, offering home delivery of products free or at a minimal charge will also help them squeeze out extra margins as people prefer to buy from nearby stores rather than drive to far-off locations. In a way, the ability to succeed for this class of SME now incrementally depends on its ability to find a niche and successfully service the clientele therein. If Open Network for Digital Commerce (ONDC) is able to scale successfully in India, the number of successful small business owners will burgeon. We will return to ONDC and the possibilities it creates in Chapter 1.

Electronic City as a Metaphor for India

Analogous to what happened in Electronic City post-1991, across India companies that have built highly efficient and highly profitable businesses and have engaged in prudent capital allocation over the years have benefited disproportionately. As we discuss this further in Chapter 2, India's shift from misguided socialism to pragmatic capitalism bodes well for these giant enterprises. In the final chapter of the book, we show, using data from the Income Tax department, that India's 600 most profitable companies account for 62 per cent of the country's profits.

At the opposite end of the spectrum, every year around 10,000 SMEs are shutting down in India[16]. Once upon a time, smaller companies used to be able to survive on tax evasion at multiple levels (payroll taxes, indirect taxes, direct taxes on profits and direct taxes on the proprietor's income). With the rise of UPI, GST and India Stack, tax evasion has become increasingly difficult for smaller companies. After payment of full taxes, it is harder for these companies to compete with their larger competitors who have the best talent, the cheapest capital, the cheapest land and the greatest access to the corridors of power. We will return to this subject in the final chapter of this book.

Summary

Three decades ago, the fortunes of two tiny villages around 20 km from the city centre of Bangalore changed for the better. In 1992, Infosys set up its campus in these villages and triggered their transformation into what is now known as Electronic City. This monumental change created winners (the tech companies, their employees, landowners) and losers (landless farmers, some SME owners). An understanding of who these winners and losers are can help explain much of what is happening in India today.

Section 1

Introduction

1

How India Changed Its Master Narrative

When I was a practising manager, I learnt more about high performance from our new assistant security guard than from the two summers I spent at the Advanced Management Program at Harvard Business School. We called him Kawade—no one was quite sure if it was his first or last name. He appeared one evening at our office at 5:30 p.m. to man the night shift. He was from a small town in Western Maharashtra, where he had completed tenth grade. He didn't know much English, and we laughed at the way he mispronounced our company's name.

Kawade had a childlike curiosity and learnt quickly how the office functioned. In the first few days he picked up how to make tea and coffee . . . Even though he didn't know much English, he learnt to operate the telex machine . . . The same went for the switchboard. Between his security duties, he could be found answering the company phone after hours. Before long, with his enquiring mind, he trained himself to operate the film projector . . .

I got a taste of Kawade's magic late one evening when I needed to speak urgently to our finance director. I knew he was travelling but wasn't sure how to reach him. Kawade made a few calls, discovered that he was staying at the Ashok Hotel in Delhi and connected me to him within minutes. If you needed anything after hours, the mantra became, 'Ask Kawade!' As a result, I noticed that people began to stay later at work because our office seemed to function more efficiently after hours than during the day.

Nine months after Kawade arrived, our telephone operator had to go on maternity leave. I learnt through the grapevine that Kawade had requested to fill in for her temporarily—he said he was tired of working at night. The personnel manager refused flatly, saying that ours was a multinational company that received calls from all over the world. How could he, with his poor English, answer incoming calls when he couldn't even pronounce the company's name correctly? I gently suggested that we try out Kawade for a few days ...

So Kawade had a new job. A few days later, our company lawyer asked me in passing if we had acquired a new EPABX system (which expands to Electronic Private Automatic Branch Exchange, a business telephone system). I looked at him quizzically.

'Your phone is now answered promptly on the second ring; earlier I had to hold on till the fifth or sixth ring.'

I smiled and told him that Kawade was our new EPABX system.

As I was going for lunch, I stopped by at Kawade's booth and asked him, 'Why do you answer the phone so promptly?'

He gave a reply that took my breath away. 'There may be a customer at the other end,' he said, 'and we might lose an order.'

Kawade brought the same curiosity, a bias for smart improvisation, a positive energy and an attitude of service to the daytime office. He quietly went on to become a role model and gradually transformed the atmosphere around him. Eventually, this modest, self-effacing, non-English-speaking non-graduate rose to great heights in our company. The lesson I learnt from Kawade's success is that attitude often matters more than skill or intelligence in creating a high-performance organization . . . You can teach skills but not attitudes, which are formed early in life.

—Gurcharan Das, quoted in *The Victory Project: Six Steps to Peak Potential,* by Saurabh Mukherjea and Anupam Gupta

Exhibit 1.1: Amul's changing advertisements—from 1960 and 2023—exemplify the change in India's master narrative

Source: Twitter, NDTV Food; images used only for illustration purposes, their copyrights remain with their respective creators and/or brand

Chess exemplifies how India's narrative is changing

On 21 April 2024, a seventeen-year old student from Velammal Vidyalaya school, Mel Ayanambakkam, Chennai, rocked the world. The son of medical doctors from the Godavari delta region of Andhra stood on the cusp of greatness[1] and this is how the *New York Times* reported the youngster's achievement:

The Next Winner of the World Chess Championship Could Be the Youngest Ever

Dommaraju Gukesh, a 17-year-old grandmaster from India, is the youngest player ever to win the Candidates Tournament.

By Dylan Loeb McClain
April 24 2024

Dommaraju Gukesh, a 17-year-old Indian grandmaster, made history on Sunday: He won the Candidates Tournament in Toronto, held to select the challenger for the World Chess Championship in the classical time control. With that achievement, he became the youngest player ever to qualify for the title match . . .

Minutes after his victory, Mr Gukesh was tired but understandably happy . . . "The way that I handled myself during the event and the way that I played my games — it was really something that I am happy about," he said. "The mental state that I achieved wasn't something that I had really expected." But, he added, "I think that I have really improved in the last one year and in the last few months."

Mr Gukesh will play Ding Liren, the reigning champion from China, in a title match . . .

There were eight elite players in the competition, including Fabiano Caruana and Hikaru Nakamura of the United States, ranked Nos. 2 and 3 in the world, and Ian Nepomniachtchi of Russia, No. 7, who was the runner-up in the last two world title matches. Those three players tied for second, a half point behind Mr. Gukesh . . .

Among those who doubted his chances was Magnus Carlsen, a former world champion. "I cannot imagine him winning," Mr. Carlsen said of Mr. Gukesh in a video recorded with David Howell, an English grandmaster, just before the competition began. "He is not quite ready yet to make a leap, and I think it is more likely that he has a bad event than a good event," he added . . .'[2]

As India celebrated Gukesh's triumph, the discussion in our company cafeteria focused not on his youth (having seen a sixteen-year Sachin Tendulkar tear into a Pakistani bowling attack in 1989, our generation is accustomed to seeing young Indians take on the world) but on what he said after winning. Gukesh told the Indian Express, 'I came to Toronto with the only intention of winning. Nothing else . . . I knew this was going to be a tough challenge. But I knew if I was going to be at my absolute best, if I do all the right things, I would have every chance.'[3]

This self-assurance isn't unique to Gukesh. In fact, it is symptomatic of this generation of Indian Grandmasters. In 1988, Vishwanathan Anand became the first Indian to become a Grandmaster. In 2002, Koneru Hampy became the first Indian woman to become a Grandmaster. By 2014, India had thirty-five Grandmasters of which thirty-three were men.[4]

By 2024, this number has burgeoned to eighty-five Grandmasters—broadly the same number as China and the United States (only Russia has more Grandmasters than these nations). Of these eighty-five Grandmasters, three are women. Out of the world's top ten male chess players, three are Indians. Out of the world's top hundred male chess players, nine are Indians.[5] In fact, for the first time ever, the world has a pair of siblings—Vaishali Rameshbabu and Praggnanandhaa Rameshbabu—both of whom are Grandmasters.[6] Vishwanathan Anand predicts that in the not too distant future, Indians will be playing each other in the chess World Championship finals.[7]

The shape and pattern of India's rise in the world of elite chess mirrors the changes taking place in the country at large:

- The number of Indian chess Grandmasters is growing at 9 per cent per annum, significantly ahead of the country's long term economic growth rate.
- The vast majority of India's chess Grandmasters hail from peninsular India.
- Almost all of India's chess Grandmasters hail from middle-class homes with the parents of these chess prodigies tending to be cerebral white-collar professionals of modest means.
- On the face of it, the involvement of the Indian state in this chess revolution has been minimal. The government, for example, does not offer subsidies or grants to chess players. Neither does it provide subsidized electricity, accommodation or training to these players.

The chess legend Garry Kasparov has called India's rise in the world of chess an 'earthquake . . . a shifting of the tectonic plates in the chess world'. So, how on earth are middle class Indian families of modest means underwriting an earthquake?[8]

The First Few Decades Post-Independence

In 2016, two psychologists, Kate McLean and Moin Syed, defined the term 'master narratives' in the following manner: [9]

> We propose that the concept of master narratives provides a framework for understanding the nature of this intersection between self and society. Master narratives are culturally shared stories that tell us about a given culture, and provide guidance for how to be a 'good' member of a culture; they are a part of the structure of society. As individuals construct a

personal narrative, they negotiate with and internalize these master narratives – they are the material they have to work with to understand how to live a good life.

In the first few decades post-Independence, India's master narrative was built around 3Fs:

- Failure, as exemplified by the hammering that China handed out to us in the 1962 war,[10] or by the country's failure to generate per capita GDP growth north of 2 per cent.
- Frustration, in the matter of generating employment, as exemplified by the Naxalite violence which swept across the eastern, central and parts of southern India from the late 1960s onwards. Famines in 1966–67[11] ravaged India and served as a recurrent reminder of the medieval state of India's economy in those harrowing early decades post-Independence.
- Fear, of not just losing one's means of earning a living but also of losing one's life as wave after wave of terrorist attacks hit the country from the early 1970s onwards when the Naxalite uprising began. When the Naxalite insurgency abated in the 1980s, the terrorist movement in Punjab gathered steam. When that abated, Kashmir became the new valley of fear.

The stifling socialism of the 'licence raj', where private capital was dissuaded from being employed in the economy, was partly to blame for these ills. The result was a nation perpetually low in confidence, which manifested in sub-optimal outcomes, not just economically but in all spheres of life. This dire state of the country prompted the best Indian minds to migrate to the West at the first available opportunity. A massive scramble then ensued amongst those who stayed back to land a 'government job', largely to have some sense of certainty about one's place in the world.

The 180-Degree Turnaround of the Last Two Decades

Fast-forward three decades to 2024, and India is the only large stock market in the world to have a twenty-year $-return CAGR approaching 13 per cent (see the table below).

Table 1.1: India's Stock Market Returns More than 13 Per Cent in US Dollar terms in Last Twenty Years

Country	TSR (30Y)	TSR (20Y)	TSR (10Y)	Rank (30Y)	Rank (20Y)	Rank (10Y)
US	10.8%	10.3%	12.8%	1	3	1
India	8.2%	13.1%	10.1%	5	1	3
Australia	9.1%	9.8%	5.8%	2	4	6
Canada	8.5%	7.7%	4.3%	4	5	8
Hong Kong	5.8%	5.4%	0.7%	8	12	12
Taiwan	7.0%	11.3%	12.6%	6	2	2
Brazil	6.2%	6.1%	-0.8%	7	10	13
China	8.7%	6.8%	4.5%	3	8	7
UK	5.7%	5.1%	2.7%	9	13	10
South Korea	3.5%	7.5%	2.2%	12	6	11
France	5.0%	6.3%	6.0%	10	9	5
Germany	4.6%	7.1%	3.8%	11	7	9
Japan	2.0%	6.0%	7.1%	13	11	4

Source: Bloomberg. All returns in the table shown below are in US$; TSR stands for 'Total Shareholder Returns', i.e., share price appreciation plus any dividends paid; for France and Germany (CAC and DAX respectively) data taken from 1st Jan 1999 when Euro was adopted; Brazil (IBOV) data taken from 1st July 1994 when Rial was adopted; all returns in USD terms; data as of June 2024

Not only is India the best-performing large stock market in the world over the past two decades, but it is also, by some distance, the fastest-growing large economy in the world. As *The Economist* said in its issue of 13 May 2022:[12]

> . . . a novel confluence of forces stands to transform India's economy over the next decade, improving the lives of 1.4bn people and changing the balance of power in Asia . . . As the country emerges from the pandemic, however, a new pattern of growth is visible. It is unlike anything you have seen before . . . These changes . . . help explain why India is forecast to be the world's fastest-growing big economy in 2022 and why it has a chance of holding on to that title for years.

Table 1.2: The World's 10 Largest Economies with their YoY Growth Rates for 2023

Rank & Country	GDP (USD billion)	GDP growth (annual)
#1 United States Of America (U.S.A)	28,781	5%
#2 China	18,533	5%
#3 Germany	4,591	3%
#4 Japan	4,110	-2%
#5 India	3,937	10%
#6 United Kingdom (U.K.)	3,495	5%
#7 France	3,130	3%
#8 Brazil	2,331	7%
#9 Italy	2,328	3%
#10 Canada	2,242	5%

Source: International Monetary Fund; GDP growth rate is annual GDP growth rate for the country for that year; both GDP and growth rate are in nominal terms (as of April 2024)

Leaving aside stock market and economic metrics, a range of events captures the change in the psyche of the nation. In August 2023, the Indian Space Research Organization (ISRO) successfully soft-landed its lander module Vikram and rover Pragyaan on the lunar South Pole, making India the only country to successfully land on the dark side of the moon. In 2023, for the first time in the Asian Games, India won over 100 medals.

In November 2023, forty-one labourers working in the Silkyara Barkot tunnel in Uttarakhand were trapped in a landslide. Over the next sixteen days, five agencies of the state and Central governments[13] deployed over 600 employees in what came to be called 'Operation Zindagi' to help dig these trapped workers out. When these employees failed to rescue the workers, the government turned to Australian tunnelling expert, Arnold Dix. As the effort reached it final stages with Dix's guidance, the main drilling machine being used for the rescue completely broke down, necessitating the recourse to a novel method. To be specific, the final leg of this remarkable seventeen-day rescue mission was performed by rat-hole miners from one of the poorest parts of one of the poorest states in India:

> A group of six skilled miners from Jhansi, Uttar Pradesh today successfully dug a safe passage to rescue workers trapped inside the Silkyara tunnel in Uttarkashi after high-tech American machines failed. These miners, known for their expertise in manual excavation, manually dig their way through the debris, covering a distance of 10–12 meters to reach the trapped workers. They rescued the workers in nearly 24 hours.[14]

Table 1.3: India's Rise Over Different Eras Post-Independence

Eras in the Indian Economy	Sensex CAGR (%)	Avg real GDP growth (%)	USD-INR exchange rate
Era 1: 1947-1979	NA	3.8%^	-0.3%*
Era 2: 1980-1990	19.70%	4.60%	8.60%
Era 3: 1991-2013	13.50%	6.60%	4.00%
Era 4: 2014-2023	12.60%	5.80%	3.00%

Source: Bloomberg; ^ - average calculated from 1952, the first year for when GDP growth rate was available; *-CAGR calculated from 1973 to 1980; for Sensex, financial year end considered; for GDP growth, calendar year end considered; for USD-INR exchange rate calendar year end considered except for 2024, for which data as of 30th June 2024 was considered.

All of this begs the question, 'How did India change its Master Narrative?'

We believe there are three reasons that led to this shift:

India is a safer and more secure country to live in than earlier

- Reduced Violence and Terrorism in the Country: Fear of violent attacks, of crime and of terrorism, has reduced significantly in India as the number of fatalities from violent events, insurgencies and terrorist movements has declined (see exhibit below). This has not only created a secure atmosphere for citizens to live in, but it has also reduced the economic costs required to counteract such events. We believe this is one of the key reasons for the change in the mind-set of the people. Indians are now embracing entrepreneurship and taking risks because they have greater physical and mental security than they did in the twentieth century.

Exhibit 1.2: Number of Violence-Related Fatalities Among Civilians And Security Forces are at an All-Time Low[15]

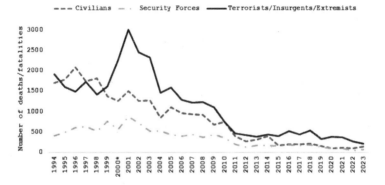

Source: South Asia Terrorism Portal; data recorded until 18 December 2023; *Data since 6 March 2000; for data from 1994–1999: Data does not include Fatalities in Left-wing Extremism; Data compiled from news reports and is provisional

- **The Creation of Attractive Employment Opportunities in the Private Sector:** Over the years, the typical preference of the Indian middle class has shifted from having a stable government job (with clarity regarding housing and pension benefits) to taking up more rewarding roles in the private sector. This is evident in the falling headcount figures in public-sector undertakings (PSUs) over the years (see exhibit below).

Exhibit 1.3: The Number of People Working for PSUs Has
Reduced Sharply Over the Past Decade

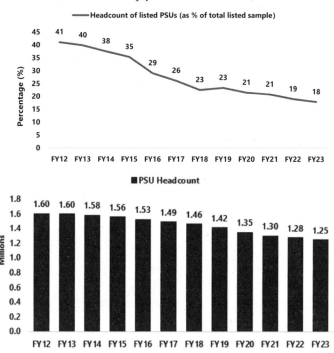

Source: Jefferies

In fact, rather than working in PSUs, ambitious Indians are
either launching their own companies or choosing to work in
start-ups. 150,000 companies[16] were launched in FY22 against
just 23,000 companies[17] launched annually twenty years ago;
in contrast only around 10,000 MSMEs are shutting down
each year. Increasingly Indians are shedding their shackles of
insecurity and diving head-first into 'making a life' and not just
'making a living', as Gurcharan Das has aptly put it in his book
Another Sort of Freedom—A Memoir (2023).

- The Rise of Hitherto Suppressed Sections of Society: The last three decades have seen people across all echelons of the Indian society—including those subjected to abuse and repression for centuries—ascending as far as their social and economic standing is concerned. This has been evident in:

The Rise of Education Among the Historically Oppressed Castes: Improved access to opportunity and changes in social perception has led to the historically oppressed castes faring far better in education (especially in higher education) today than thirty or forty years ago. Even more encouragingly, women from these castes have pulled far ahead of their male counterparts, with the gender parity index (GPI) exceeding 1 around five years ago and staying there consistently (see exhibit below). (Note: GPI is a measure of the number of women enrolling in higher education for every man enrolling. A GPI in excess of 1 indicates that more women than men are getting educated).

Exhibit 1.4: The Gender Parity Index (Which Measures the Ratio of Girls to Boys Enrolled in Higher Education) has Gone up for the Historically Deprived Castes

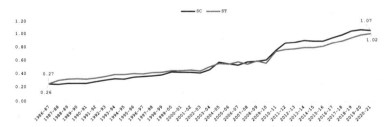

Source: EPW Research Foundation, All India Survey of Higher Education (AISHE); Data from 1986–87 to 2010–1, taken from EPWRF (1986–87 to 2006–07) from Selected Educational Statistics; 2007–08 to 2009–10 from Statistics of Higher and Technical Education; and from 2011–12 onwards from AISHE documents.

Reduction in Caste-Related Wage Gap in Blue-Collar Jobs: Researchers at Azim Premji University have observed caste convergence in some if not all categories of workplaces. For instance, the gap between other backward classes (OBCs) and upper castes has reduced significantly, with the former moving incrementally into services and manufacturing. Members from the scheduled castes (SCs), on the other hand, have shifted out of agriculture (i.e., they are no longer oppressed by zamindars and landowners) and into the construction sector.[18]

In fact, according to Ashwini Deshpande of Ashoka University and Rajesh Ramachandran of Heidelberg University, caste-based wage disparity has become almost non-existent (i.e., wages have converged) for below-median salary earners, but not so in jobs that pay above median salary.[19]

Economic Policy Reforms Have Been Gradual and Very Effective

The year 1991 marked a paradigm shift in India's policymaking with the liberalization of the economy and the ending of the 'license raj'. As we explain in Chapter 3, for those of us who lived through the momentous summer of 1991, it was an unforgettable time. In the space of two months, Prime Minister Narasimha Rao and Finance Minister Manmohan Singh used the then dire balance-of-payments crisis to leave behind four decades of socialism and open up the Indian economy, both to the private sector and to foreigners. After four decades of believing that foreigners would 'drain' India, India's policymakers—under pressure from the International Monetary Fund (IMF) and the World Bank—opened up the Indian economy to foreign investors. After four decades of trying to prop up public-sector units to build the Indian economy, the government now allowed the private sector to invest in most sectors of the economy.

India's economic reforms continued after 1991 at a more gradual pace. For instance, in 1991, foreign direct investment (FDI) was allowed in India, though limited to 51 per cent of the shareholding. Today, more than thirty years later, the FDI limit for most sectors has been revised to 100 per cent. The result, unsurprisingly, is increased FDI inflows into the country over the years, as evidenced by the exhibit below.

Exhibit 1.5: Increased FDI Inflows (2013–23)

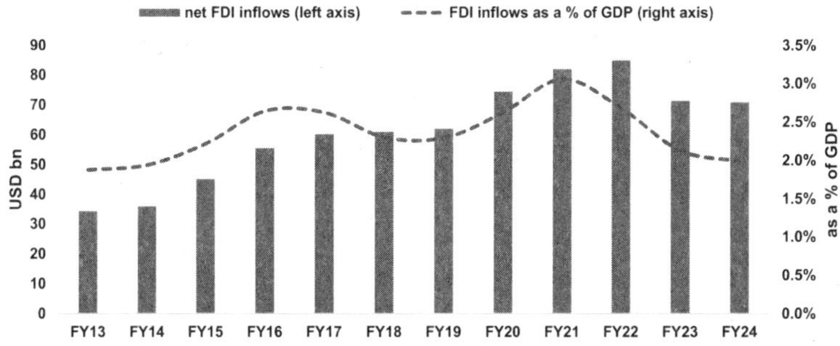

Source: GDP figures from Bloomberg and Net FDI Inflows from Statista; figures are in USD bn and those for FY23 and FY24 (net FDI inflow) are estimates.

As the founders of Marcellus, the firm which employs us, will testify, starting a new business in India and doing business in India are now easier than ever before. While more can be done on this front, the nation's improvement is tangible, especially in comparison to how the rest of the world has shaped up in this century.

Exhibit 1.6: Improved Ease-of-Doing-Business Ranking for India

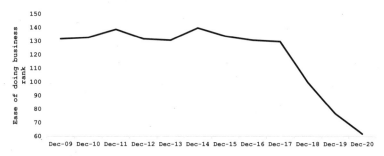

Source: Bloomberg (sourced from World Bank); the metric got discontinued after 2020, and therefore there is no data recorded for the years thereafter.

In addition, both corporate tax rates and income tax rates for low-income earners have fallen sharply over the past decade (see exhibit below).

Exhibit 1.7: Indian Corporate Taxes Go Down
(from 60 per cent to 25 per cent)

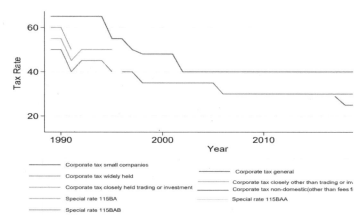

Source: CMIE (sourced from research document from National Institute of Public Finance and Policy)

The combination of lower corporate tax rates, GST (which was introduced in 2017) and India Stack (discussed in more detail in the final section of this chapter) has meant that: (a) the incentive to evade taxes has reduced; and (b) it has become easier for authorities to catch tax evaders, courtesy the electronic trails created by the GST payment system. This in turn has meant that over the past couple of years, tax collections have grown faster than nominal GDP growth (20 per cent vs 17 per cent).

A further beneficial effect of reduced tax evasion is the financialization of savings. As per RBI data, 95 per cent of Indian household savings are in physical assets—real estate, land and gold.[20] Historically, one of the reasons Indian households have preferred physical savings was that it was easier to park black money in physical assets. However, over the past twenty years, these physical assets have struggled to beat inflation after taking taxes into account. In other words, physical assets have not created wealth in real terms.

On the other hand, with the ubiquity of mobile phones and the application of Aadhar and UPI, not only has information regarding financial assets become easy to access, setting up an account and investing have also become paperless and relatively straightforward. Combine this with the stellar run that the Indian stock market has had over the past decade, (the Nifty has compounded at 13 per cent per annum over the past decade), and you have a recipe for a boom in financial assets.

To give a sense of the scale at which financialization is playing out in India, it is worth looking at the following numbers:

- The number of demat accounts in India has grown ten times over the past decade to 160 MN.

- The number of mutual fund folios in India has grown three and a half times over the past decade to over 145 million.

Annual equity inflows into Indian mutual funds have risen from Rs 20,000 crore per year a decade ago to roughly Rs 1.6 lakh crore per year currently, i.e., an 8x rise (23 per cent CAGR).

The annual gross premiums written by life insurers has risen from Rs 2.8 lakh crore per year a decade ago to roughly Rs 7 lakh crore a year now, a two and a half times rise (9 per cent CAGR).

The annual gross premiums written by general insurers has risen from Rs 74,000 crore per year a decade ago to roughly Rs 2.5 lakh crore per year now, a three and a half times rise (13 per cent CAGR).

Add to that the roughly Rs 1.8 lakh crore flowing in every year into the National Pension Scheme (NPS) and Employee Provident Fund (EPF), and you can see that each year Indian households are investing roughly Rs 13 lakh crore into the Indian financial system. A decade ago, this figure was just Rs 4 lakh crore a year, i.e., over the past decade, **annual financial inflows (from Indian households) into the financial system have tripled**.

Rs 13 lakh crore is $160 bn per year. That's the amount of annual financial inflows from Indian households into the Indian financial system.

Naturally, rapid financialization of savings has resulted in the cost of capital dropping, and one can see this both in the cost at which the Indian sovereign finances its deficit in the bond market—see exhibit below—and in the cost of equity, leading to greater participation in equities.

Exhibit 1.8: Falling Cost of Funds, Rising Market Participation with Easing Policy Environment

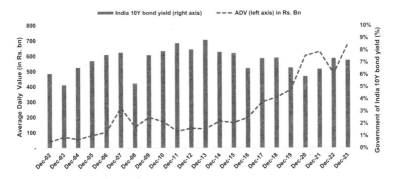

Source: Average Daily Value (ADV) Traded from Ace Equity and 10-year government bond yield from Bloomberg; 3 month moving average used for ADV; BSE 500 index used for ADV calculation.

Deployment of Technology for the Benefit of Indians Far and Wide

Technology in its various shapes and forms has transformed the way humanity has gone about conducting its life. Prior to the industrial revolution, across the world the production of manufactured goods was largely done in the homes of contracted workers. In the eighteenth century, industrial technology revolutionized production and paved the way for the creation of factories i.e. centralized locations where large machines were installed and where workers would congregate to use the machines to produce manufactured goods. in the late twentieth and early twenty-first centuries, the widespread use of computers and the Internet increased the efficiency of workers in factories and offices multi-fold.

Interestingly, in all these instances, the economic upside of technology adoption was found to be the greatest when these benefits were shared across all sections of the economy—i.e., not just among the owner-industrialist class but also among the worker class. In the eighteenth century, initially the factory owners were the clear beneficiaries of the newly introduced industrial technologies. However, as workers became skilled in their use of machinery, their efficiency increased and so did their incomes. In the twentieth century, the Western economies reaped the benefits of another bout of technology innovation centred on the use of computers and automation in the factory and in the office.

As Daron Acemoglu and Simon Johnson have pointed out in *Power and Progress: Our Thousand-Year Struggle over Technology and Prosperity* (2023):

> After World War II, much of the Western world, and some countries in Asia, built new institutions supporting shared prosperity and enjoyed rapid growth that benefited almost all segments of their societies. The decades following 1945 came to be referred in France as the 'les trente glorieuses,' the thirty glorious years, and the feeling was widespread throughout the Western world. This growth had two critical building blocks, similar to those that had begun to emerge in the United Kingdom during the second half of the nineteenth century: first, a direction of travel for new technology that generated not just cost savings through automation but also plenty of new tasks, products, and opportunities; and second, an institutional structure that bolstered countervailing powers from workers and government regulation.

Over the past twenty years, tech visionaries in India like Nandan Nilekani have teamed up with policymakers to bring the benefits of technology to the masses in the country. The overall set of tech innovations—called 'India Stack'—has been built step by step.

It began with a vision to provide all Indians with something like a social security number for identity (Aadhaar) in 2009, which was then overlaid by bank accounts for all (Jan Dhan) in 2015 and finally by massive proliferation of low-cost Internet and smartphones by 2017 (with the launch of Jio). Together, these building blocks, known as the JAM trinity, allowed 1.4 billion Indians to get an identity, a bank account and a medium with which to connect (at low cost) with the digital economy and the financial system.

The next step was to build a Unified Payments Interface (UPI), which enabled currency-less and digital transaction as well as the transfer of money, which was launched in 2016. According to the National Payments Corporation of India (NPCI), the body in charge of operating the retail payments and settlement systems in India, the total value of transactions using UPI in May 2024 in India crossed Rs 240 trillion (US$3 tn) on an annualised basis[21] or 70 per cent of the Indian GDP!

The next step in this journey is a similar infrastructure for goods and e-commerce via ONDC, which will allow all buyers and sellers on the Internet to freely transact with one another, as against what happens at present, where an Amazon customer can purchase only from vendors selling their wares on the Amazon platform, or a Flipkart customer is only able to purchase from the Flipkart platform, etc. As one would expect from this brief description of how ONDC would function by cutting across the currently siloed ecommerce ecosystem, the introduction of such a platform could potentially transform Indian ecommerce.

As Nandan Nilekani said in an interview with Livemint in November 2022:

. . . . [the] three big revolutions will be—democratizing credit through AA [Account Aggregation Framework], democratizing commerce through ONDC; and essentially making the delivery of products much simpler and cheaper with logistics' transformation. These three steps will lay the foundation for equitable commercial activity for both goods and services. India will move from a pre-paid cash informal economy to a post-paid formal cashless productive economy.

Unlike in the US, where tech has created a narrow elite of billionaires, India's story is different. Here, 'digital public goods' have been employed to benefit consumers and producers of all shapes and sizes. This has reduced transaction costs for almost every Indian, reduced working capital cycles for most businesses, made access to financial funding easier for tens of millions of low-income borrowers and SMEs and enabled the sovereign to collect taxes more easily.

Investment Implications

As Vladimir Lenin[22] has said, 'There are decades where nothing happens; and there are weeks where decades happen.' In the first few decades post-Independence, nothing much happened in India from the perspective of this vast nation's master narrative. In the twenty-first century, however, India is beginning to make up for those difficult decades.

What India has found at long last is a flywheel where a combination of incentives, enforcement and modern tech drives tax collections (at a faster rate than GDP growth). That in turn allows the sovereign to finance infrastructure. In parallel, thanks to the same flywheel, savings are financialized (rather than being put in low-yielding physical assets). This lowers the cost of capital, which in turn makes it easier for companies to fund themselves and drive capex. That capex in turn drives GDP growth. And thus the virtuous cycle continues.

Summary

Master narratives are culturally shared stories that guide the thoughts and behaviours of a community of people, here the citizens of a country. After surviving the dark, desperate decades immediately following Independence, India has reinvented its master narrative over the past twenty years. The world-beating performance of the Nifty50 over the last twenty years, the euphoria of the Chandrayaan landing on the dark side of the moon, the gutsy resolve shown during the Silkyara tunnel rescue, the cerebral triumphs of India's chess grandmasters and the world-leading GDP growth clocked in the post-Covid era, all point to the creation of a new, more confident and more determined master narrative for India. Central to this new narrative are: (a) the creation of a more secure society; (b) effective policymaking and (c) creation of digital public goods that have allowed India to finally lock into a virtuous cycle of economic prosperity.

2

A Century Spent Answering Four Questions

Exhibit 2.1: Four Twentieth Century Economic Thinkers[1]

Note: from left to right, Dadabhai Naoroji, Mahadev Govind Ranade, Gopal Krishna Gokhale, and Mahatma Gandhi

India did not possess well-developed capital and labour markets in the nineteenth century. It did have cheap labour, cheap material, and community-bound entrepreneurial resources, but the capital was expensive, large-scale labour markets non-existent, transportation costs of material high, and the merchants did not understand machinery. India's colonial connection was instrumental in overcoming these barriers to industrialization.

—Tirthankar Roy, in *The Economic History of India, 1857 to 2010* (Fourth edition, 2020).

Introduction

Over the past century, Indian political discourse has taken many turns in its approach to policymaking. The socialist and redistributive set-up (of the pre-1980 era) has given way to an infrastructure-focused capex-heavy one (under the current dispensation). Multiple dispensations at the Centre have, to this end, advocated both verbally and via policy actions, what they felt the economic discourse in the country should ideally be, with the last decade witnessing exceptional infrastructure development.

The critical questions around economic policymaking that ought to be debated in any vibrant, free-market economy, were first raised by four towering personalities at the beginning of the twentieth century. They were Dadabhai Naoroji (1825–1917), Mahadev Govind Ranade (1842–1901), Gopal Krishna Gokhale (1866–1915) and Mahatma Gandhi (1869–1948).

The table below captures the essence of the questions these thinkers posed to India's freedom fighters in the years prior to Independence. And, post-1947, India's policymakers have continued to wrestle with these four questions (with varying degrees of success in finding answers to them).

Table 2.1: Four Pertinent Questions Raised by Four Great Thinkers

Thinker	Date of Birth and Death	Key Question
Dadabhai Naoroji	4th September 1825 – 30th June 1917	Can India 'gain' from global trade OR will the world 'drain' India much like the East India Company and the Crown did?
MG Ranade	18th January 1842 – 16th January 1901	Can the free market deliver economic development OR does the Government have to do the job?
GK Gokhale	9th May 1866 – 19th February 1915	Should India focus on educating & skilling its people OR should the Govt just focus on 'hard' public goods like infrastructure & defence?
Mahatma Gandhi	2nd October 1869 – 30th January 1948	Should India focus on developing sectors where it has comparative advantages in the global economy (e.g., IT Services) OR should India try to be self-sufficient (Atmanirbhar) and build out sectors where it does NOT

Source: Marcellus Investment Managers

To give you a sense of the immense intellectual depth required to pose such questions in the colonized India of a century ago, John Maynard Keynes's definitive book on economic policymaking, *The General Theory of Employment, Interest and Money*, the first clear guide to how nations should think about managing their economy and their finances, was published only in 1936. Long before that, and several decades before macroeconomics became an academic discipline in the universities of the West, the four Indian thinkers had thought about the four critical issues that sit at the heart of modern economic policymaking.

In this chapter, we will discuss the origins of the four questions asked by these thinkers. In the next chapter, we will look at how various Indian governments have answered the same four questions in utterly divergent ways, and in so doing changed the course of the Indian economy and the fortunes of various sectors.

For instance, P.V. Narasimha Rao's and Manmohan Singh's decision to open up the Indian economy to the world at large in July 1991 transformed the prospects of India's IT services sector and directly resulted in the burgeoning of giant Indian IT services companies like TCS (now the world's second largest IT services firm) and Infosys. However, the same policy decision put paid to the prospects of India's then largest domestic car manufacturers, Hindustan Motors and

Premier Automobiles (both of whom were part of the Sensex in 1991).

In a similar vein, the National Democratic Alliance's (NDA's) decision to incentivize self-sufficiency (Atmanirbharta) through production-linked incentives (PLI) has resulted in the creation of a burgeoning Electric Vehicle (EV) two-wheeler industry[2] in India while diminishing the growth prospects for manufacturers of conventional two-wheelers.

Notwithstanding these inevitable tradeoffs that riddle policymaking the world over, we believe that policy decisions are an effective way to find and evaluate answers to the core issues that underpin economic development. And so, if Indian policymaking—and the impact it has on companies' prospects—is to be understood, an understanding of the basic tenets of the aforementioned four questions becomes crucial. Let's delve further into each of the four foundational questions that were raised over a century ago.

Dadabhai Naoroji

Can India 'gain' from global trade OR will trade with the world 'drain' India?

The busiest street in downtown Mumbai, D.N. Road in Fort, is named after Dadabhai Naoroji, a leading politician who was the president of the Indian National Congress (INC) three times between 1886 and 1907. The idea he is most famously known to have developed is the 'Drain Theory', which essentially postulated that if a country has no power to stand up to its buyers/stakeholders in the global market, it is going to be a net loser from global trade.

The British, first under the East India Company (EIC) and then directly under the Crown from 1858 onwards, governed the Indian subcontinent for almost 200 years. In these couple of centuries, they left a lasting legacy in the form of the railways, the telegraph, the English language and the game of cricket. However, this was not all. There were a few who thought the British were unfairly extracting resources from India that were not to the benefit of Indians. In fact, as B.R. Tomlinson writes in his book *The Economy of Modern India: From 1860 to the Twenty First Century* (2013):

> The crucial point for the nationalists was that British rule brought about a 'drain of wealth' as India met a large deficit in goods and services with Britain, plus interest charges and capital repayments in London. Nationalists fiercely contested the assumptions on which such calculations were based, arguing in particular that India's defence establishment was designed to meet Britain's needs, and that the railways were an expensive military asset rather than an appropriate piece of developmental infrastructure.

In fact, Tomlinson went on to highlight, 'Lord Salisbury described India as "an English barrack in the Oriental seas from which we may draw any number of troops without paying for them"'[3].There is some merit in the argument against outward remittances by the British working in India that Naoroji was putting forth; foreigners worked in India and used all the resources they needed from the country but sent remittances to England, therefore draining India of what could have been spent and/or invested in India.

However, it was not only the remittances that bothered the proponents of the Drain Theory but also the relatively disadvantageous terms on which foreign trade took place between India and England. In fact, John Stuart Mill, the English philosopher and economist, had explained this succinctly in his book *Principles of Political Economy* of 1848: 'A country which makes regular (non-commercial) payments to foreign countries, besides losing what it pays, loses also something more, by the less advantageous terms on which it is forced to exchange its production for foreign commodities'[4]

Interestingly, not everyone was convinced that the Drain Theory was the primary explanation for the poverty in India. Bankim Chandra Chatterjee thought the Drain Theory was largely incorrect. He believed that, quite contrary to the 'draining' of resources from the country because of the British and the resultant introduction of formal banking systems and processes, safeguards against people losing money had been put in place. In 1892, he wrote, 'If someone wishes to save, he can be confident that he and his progeny would be able to enjoy the fruits of it.'

Furthermore, and quite contrary to the general idea that the Drain Theory had put forth, Bankim Chandra believed that an increase in trade did not mean a loss of wealth:

> If we spend 6 rupees in buying British cloth we are getting a commodity in exchange for it. If we spend more than a fair price for it, we lose. But if we cannot buy that cloth for less than Rs 6 from elsewhere the price is not unfair. Hence, the country does not lose.[5]

Therefore, while the Drain Theory as proposed by Naoroji had merit, there were other drivers of India's poverty. Furthermore, if the terms of trade (between India and the wider world) could be improved, the country could benefit from foreign trade. As a result, throughout the history of independent India, we have seen governments grappling with the question of whether India should remain a closed economy or open up to the world at large, with terms of trade that are fair from the Indian perspective (more on this in the next chapter).

Contemporaneous to Naoroji was another stalwart thinker who revolutionized not only the social discourse in the country but also made the case for massive industrialization and the resultant acceleration in growth—Mahadev Govind Ranade.

Justice Ranade

Should India pursue free-market driven economic development OR state-driven development?

> Global economic expansion and the global shift in terms of trade in favour of agriculture encouraged expansion in cultivation. The agricultural expansion was a combined story of commercialization, industrialization, and banking growth. During the colonial era, a pattern of economic change emerged in which land, trade, finance, and manufacturing became interdependent parts of a single system. Growth of trade enabled merchants to make enough money to invest in modern industry.
> —Tirthankar Roy in *The Economic History of India, 1857 to 2010* (Fourth edition, 2020).

Born in Niphad in the Nashik district of Maharashtra in 1842, Justice Mahadev Govind Ranade spent a large part of his life trying to bring social reform to India. To this end, he campaigned for widow remarriage and their emancipation by establishing the Widow Marriage Association in 1861. Justice Ranade was also instrumental in founding the Maharashtra Girls Education Society, which started one of the oldest schools in Pune for girls, the Huzurpaga. He was also a notable politician (one of the founding members of the INC), a justice at the Bombay High Court and the editor of an Anglo-Marathi daily in Bombay named *Induprakash*.

A stalwart in economic thought and way ahead of his times, Justice Ranade articulated the pressing need for capital infusion in the economy. He was of the opinion that for India to grow beyond the meagre rate that it had attained over the last few centuries, it needed to pivot away from agriculture and towards industry—towards manufacturing and capital-intensive industries specifically.

In order for this to happen, the cogs of a free-market economy had to function effectively. A free market economy primarily functions on the idea of profit maximization. If people see the chance of earning outsized profits, they will enter the market (by becoming producers), thereby driving private capex into the economy.

However, with the British introducing their mass-produced, low-cost and better-quality products in India, many homegrown Indian producers had gone out of business. Therefore, Justice Ranade explained that initially at least, industry would need government-directed capital infusion and protection to help firms gain the resources and confidence to compete with imported goods. In his inaugural address at the first industrial conference in Pune in 1890, which Ranade himself organized, he set forth the steps by which the state could help indigenous or domestic private enterprises to grow:

> While we put forth our energies in these directions, we can well count upon the assistance of the State in regulating our Co-operative efforts by helping us to form Deposit and Finance Banks, and facilitating recoveries of advances made by them, by encouraging New Industries with Guarantees and Subsidies, or loans at low interest, by pioneering the way to new Enterprises, and by affording facilities for Emigration and Immigration, and establishing Technical Institutes and buying more largely the Stores they require here and, in many cases, by producing their own Stores.[6]

Ranade believed it was essential that the country shifted from being an agrarian economy to becoming a manufacturing powerhouse driven by domestic industries if it were to grow at a healthy pace, where the state's role would be to encourage private investment but not run businesses itself.

In *A History of Economic Thought in India*, author Ajit Dasgupta summed up what Ranade stood for:

> To conclude, Ranade's approach to economic policy was guided by an over-riding objective: the development of productive capacity. This applied to agriculture as much as to industry. In both, government had a vital role to play, but its role was to initiate, encourage and allow, rather than direct, take over or control.

Gokhale

Should the Government focus on 'hard' infrastructure OR 'soft' infrastructure?

> To expect the government to be an effective agent in mass literacy would mean not only a much larger scale of investment but also a battle against social prejudices and biases that derived from caste sentiments and the low status of women in society.
>
> <div align="right">Tirthankar Roy in <i>The Economic History of India</i>,
1857–2010, (2020)</div>

Born in the coastal region of Maharashtra in Ratnagiri in 1866, Gopal Krishna Gokhale was a social reformer, a professor of political economy at Fergusson College in Pune and a politician of great repute in the pre-Independence era. He was committed to serving the underprivileged, and to this end he founded the Servants of India Society in 1905. A moderate politician, he was an active member of the INC and left an indelible mark on the political discourse by protesting against the ill-treatment of the underprivileged in India. His interest in and contributions to India's political economy are such that the famous Gokhale Institute of Political Science and Economics (GIPE) in Pune is named after him.

As a prolific thinker and eminent economist, Gokhale emphasized the need for compulsory elementary education in India. He believed that overall growth in the economy can happen only when its population is literate.

> Mass education contributes to economic growth directly because education improves the capability and productivity of human beings, and thus adds to resource endowment, and indirectly by increasing the choice of occupations, making it more likely that the person with the right aptitude for a line of work would learn and perform that work.
>
> —Tirthankar Roy in *The Economic History of India,*
> 1857–2010 (2020)

The principles of finance that Gokhale religiously believed in were quite old school but effective—the government should cut costs wherever possible and keep corporate taxes low so that private investment does not get hindered and the nation gets a chance to benefit from the fruits of private ventures. From this vantage point, he saw public spending on education as an investment by the nation in the productive capacity of its people.

More generally, Gokhale believed in giving impetus to private investment rather than in the state collecting higher taxes from private firms and then using those monies to drive development. This is evident in the following excerpt from what he said in 1902:

> The true guiding principle of Indian finance ought to be a severe economy, a rigorous retrenchment of expenditure in all branches of administration consistent with efficiency,

keeping the level of taxation as low as possible so as to leave the springs of national industry free play and room for unhampered development.[7]

With the benefit of hindsight, what both Ranade and Gokhale focused on, i.e., hard (capex on factories and machines) and soft infrastructure (human capital development), were complementary requirements for economic development. One cannot exist without the other.

Mahatma Gandhi

Should India be 'atmanirbhar' OR should it focus on Ricardian comparative advantage?

As if being the leader of India's freedom struggle wasn't enough, the Mahatma was also a deep and remarkably original thinker on the subject of the economic challenges facing India.

Mahatma Gandhi's thinking on what India needed to become a developed nation was distinct from the point of view articulated by Justice Ranade. Specifically, Gandhi wanted India to be a self-sufficient economy and to bring its rural economy to the forefront of the drive for development.

> Gandhi, on the other hand, did not regard industrialization as a goal that India should adopt. The overall vision which led Gandhi to his doctrines of the limitation of wants and swadeshi also led him to oppose modern industrial development, says
>
> Ajit Dasgupta in *A History of Economic Thoughts in India*

Presciently, even a century ago the Mahatma's primary concern was that machines would displace India's labour, leading to unemployment. Therefore, in his world view of self-reliance, where everyone benefits from the fruits of their labour, the modern model of machine-based production that was effectively the hallmark of the Industrial Revolution in Europe did not seem like one that could be usefully adopted for independent India.

Over the past seventy years, as the free-market principles propagated by liberal Western economists (the so called 'Washington Consensus', thanks to the role of the World Bank and IMF in propagating this point of view) have gained currency, policymakers the world over have veered away from self-sufficiency and focused on comparative advantage, an economic construct first articulated by David Ricardo in the year 1817.

Ricardo said that countries should produce only those goods (or services) which they are comparatively good at making (i.e., the goods that they can produce comparatively more cheaply than other countries), and then trade this for other goods with other nations. This, said Ricardo, would make all the countries involved better off (rather than each country producing everything to the best of its capacities and capabilities).

To illustrate this using an example, country A can produce 1,000 units of cakes or 3,000 units of cookies, or it could split its workers into two groups and produce 500 cakes and 1,500 cookies. Country B, on the other hand, with the same number of workers, could also produce 1,000 cakes, but if they were to make only cookies, they could produce only 2,000. Now, if both the countries decided to produce both cakes and cookies, they could produce 1,000 cakes and 2,500 cookies. However, if country B could make 1,000 cakes (enough for both the countries) and country A 3,000 cookies, the total production by two countries would be higher than what they could each produce without trade. Thus, thanks to trade, both the countries would be better off, because each country would specialize in what it does most efficiently (see exhibit below[8]).

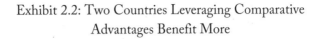

Exhibit 2.2: Two Countries Leveraging Comparative
Advantages Benefit More

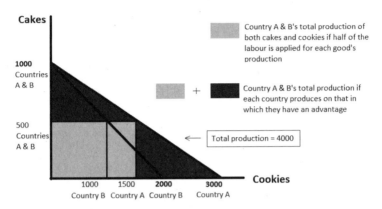

Source: Marcellus Investment Managers; grey area signifies the total production if both the countries produced both the goods and the black + grey area signifies the total production in both countries if they use comparative advantage to produce only what they are good at and import the rest; boldfaced numbers on both the axes signify maximum quantity that can be produced by each country if the other good is not produced; non-boldfaced numbers signify quantity that can be produced if half the labour force produces one good and the other half produces the other one in both the countries

Ricardo's economics of comparative advantage is in direct contradiction to Gandhi's idea of self-sufficiency. However, Ricardo's economics assumes that each country is able to negotiate fair terms of trade for itself in the global economy. The Mahatma knew from bitter experience that that is not how the world worked, especially for a British colony like India. Nearly a century later, Tomlinson summarized neatly the Mahatma's incisive understanding of the unfairness of the trade arrangements imposed on India:

Colonial rule broke down the autonomous economy of independent handicraft workers and self-sufficient peasants, and directed domestic economic activity towards two main areas – export oriented agriculture with very small returns to provide primary products for the West at bargain prices before Independence, and limited industrialization dependent on alliances with foreign firms for technology since then.[9]

In the next chapter, we will explain how different Indian governments have answered the four questions highlighted in this chapter differently. We will show how those varying answers have impacted India's economy. We will conclude by explaining how we believe the people in charge of India today are answering these four questions.

Summary

Over the past century, every politician and policymaker who has governed India has wrestled with four critical questions: (a) Can the free market deliver economic development OR does the government have to do the job? (b) Can India gain from opening itself to the wider world OR will the world act as a 'drain' on it? (c) Should India be a self-sufficient economy OR should India focus on its comparative advantages? and (d) Should the government focus on 'soft' public goods like education and healthcare OR is it enough if the government simply provides 'hard' infrastructure like roads and ports?

3

How Policymakers Have Driven Economic Change in India

. . . how we use knowledge and science depends on vision—the way that humans understand how they can turn knowledge into techniques and methods targeted at solving specific problems . . . The bad news is that even at the best of times, the visions of powerful people have a disproportionate effect on what we do with our existing tools and the direction of innovation . . . society may even become gripped by visions that favor powerful individuals. Such visions then help business and technology leaders pursue plans that increase their wealth, political power, or status. These elites may convince themselves that whatever is good for them is also best for the common good.

—Simon Johnson and Daron Acemoglu in *Power and Progress: Our Thousand-Year Struggle over Technology and Prosperity* (2023)

Exhibit 3.1: Increased Government Spending (Centre and States) over 50 Years

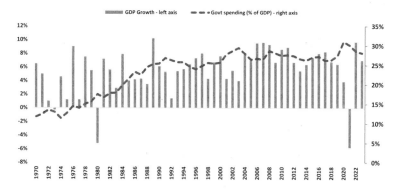

Source: Bloomberg (sourced from the International Monetary Fund database); data as of calendar year end for each of the years shown in the chart; real GDP growth used (shown by the bars)

Background

In the previous chapter, we highlighted how, over a century ago, four great thinkers—Dadabhai Naoroji, Mahadev Govind Ranade, Gopal Krishna Gokhale and Mahatma Gandhi—had captured the four issues that have been at the heart of economic policymaking in India since the country gained independence (see Table 2.1).

The attempts made by independent India's elected governments to answer these questions resulted in India's economy experiencing four distinct eras, as demarcated in the table below. In this part of the chapter, we capture the crux of what happened in each era.

Behold the Leviathan

Table 3.1: India's Rise after Independence

Eras in the Indian Economy	Sensex CAGR (%)	Avg real GDP growth (%)	USD-INR exchange rate CAGR (%)
Era 1: 1947-1979	NA	3.8%^	-0.3%*
Era 2: 1980-1990	19.7%	4.6%	8.6%
Era 3: 1991-2013	13.5%	6.6%	4.0%
Era 4: 2014-2023	11.4%	5.6%	3.2%

Source: Bloomberg; ^ - average calculated from 1952, the first year for when GDP growth rate was available; *-CAGR calculated from 1973 to 1980; for Sensex, financial year end considered; for GDP growth, calendar year end considered; for USD-INR exchange rate calendar year end considered except for 2024, for which data as of 30th June 2024 was considered.

If you don't have the time to read how the four eras played out for India, the table below summarizes Indian policymakers' response to the four central questions in the first seven decades of India's independence:

Table 3.2: Government Response to Questions Raised by Four Great Indian Thinkers[1]

Time periods	Q1: Open the country OR close the country to global trade?	Q2: Minimalist state OR total control state?	Q3: Soft capex OR hard capex?	Q4: Self-sufficiency OR comparative advantage?
Era 1 (1947 to 1979)	Closed economy with negligible external trade	Total state-controlled industries and enterprises	Investment in education with IITs and IIMs set up	Thrust on self-sufficient economy with import substitution
Era 2 (1980 to 1990)	Limited opening-up of the economy for trade	Still a majorly government-controlled ecosystem	Deregulation was the focus so no particular emphasis on soft capex, like on education	Self-sufficiency was still the dominant strategy whilst comparative-advantage ideas had started getting discussed
Era 3 (1991 to 2013)	Economy was opened to the world by the reforms of 1991	State had materially started relinquishing its control to let free-market forces drive the economy	Education and softer aspects of capex were still not the focus even in this era	Slowly, the idea of comparative advantage had started gaining ground, especially with the burgeoning IT services sector
Era 4 (2014 to date)	Economy has been fully opened to global competitive forces barring 2-3 strategic industries like railways and defence	State has relinquished most if not all control over business, with incremental divestments in PSUs (like Air India)	New Education Policy was introduced in 2020. However, government spending on education has stayed at sub-5% of GDP	Comparative advantage now drives trade flows except in protected sectors like agriculture and defence and in sectors where the government is pursuing self-sufficiency using production-linked incentives

A knowledge of the evolution of the country during these four eras is key to understanding how India's policymakers have intervened time and again in the economy, and their impact on it. From our perspective as investors in the Indian stock market, the key implications of this policy analysis are the forward-looking changes that we believe are likely to play out. We have listed the four eras and their policy implications next, followed by the changes we see coming in the years ahead.

Era 1: Full-Throttle Socialism and the
'License Raj' (1947–1979)

For a flavour of what life was like in pre-1980 India, we begin with an anecdote from the celebrated writer Gurcharan Das's latest book, *Another Sort of Freedom—a Memoir* (2023):

> There was a flu epidemic in India. As a result, sales of the entire line of Vicks cough and cold products shot through the roof. The factory workers worked overtime to meet the demand. At the end of the season, the company declared record profits. Everyone was happy, except the legal department. The company secretary, with fear in his eyes, came to my room, accompanied by two lawyers with long faces. Our sales had exceeded the production capacity authorized in our official licence. We had broken the law, and it might mean a jail sentence. They wanted my help to draft a defence. From heroes we had become criminals, and a pall of gloom descended on the office.
>
> Sure enough, we received a summons from Delhi. It was a preliminary hearing, but I had to be present. Two lawyers accompanied me to the joint secretary's office, where we were made to wait for hours. The officer was reading a

newspaper as we entered. He gave a cold look that said he didn't want to be disturbed. I was afraid but tried not to show it. Eventually, he looked up.

'What?' he asked impatiently.

One of the lawyers handed him a copy of the summons. He glanced at it irritably. 'What?' he repeated. I explained nervously that the flu epidemic had resulted in extra demand for our products. We had merely done our duty in keeping the shelves stocked at pharmacies. Our products had come to the rescue of millions of mothers whose children had suffered from the flu.

He stopped me, irritation showing in his voice. 'But you have broken the law!' he thundered. I replied politely that something was wrong with the law that punished one for producing things that had benefited millions of sick people. Anywhere else, one would be applauded for treating the sick, especially children. The joint secretary pushed his chair back noisily, signalling the end of the interview. We had broken the law, and the law would now take its course.

As I reached the door, I don't know what came over me. I turned around defiantly and asked him how our country would appear to the world if news got out that our government had punished the executive of a foreign company for helping to produce products that alleviated peoples' misery during an epidemic. Imagine such a story on page 3 of the *New York Times*.

'Are you threatening me?' he thundered.

'No, sir. I was merely appealing to your common sense as a fellow citizen. By punishing us, you'd be making our prime minister a laughing stock of the world outside.' He gave me a venomous look and gestured me to get out of his office.

Instances like these were the norm rather than the exception during this time period. India had only recently gained independence and had been bloodied not just by Partition in 1947, but also by a war with China (in 1962), and then by two successive wars with Pakistan (in 1965 and 1971). These wars had sapped the impoverished Indian economy of the meagre resources it possessed after 200 years of extractive colonial rule by the British.

As a result, echoing Dadabhai Naoroji, India's policymaking elite was utterly convinced during this era that global integration would function as a 'drain' on India. Thus, the decision was taken to 'close' the Indian economy to foreigners and to let the government control the 'commanding heights' of the economy—i.e., critical sectors like mineral resources, metals, insurance, banking, machine tools, electricals, etc., would be controlled by the state via public-sector undertakings (PSUs). The result was paltry external trade, a fixed exchange rate (fixed obviously at a rate which overvalued the Indian rupee), GDP growth of 3.5 per cent per annum and per capita income growth of 1 per cent per annum.

Famines (1966–67)[2], civil strife (the Naxal uprising began in 1967 in north Bengal and then spread through eastern and southern India through the 1970s) and the imposition of Emergency (1975–77) destroyed the hopes and dreams of a generation of Indians. Access to capital and access to the new political elite (who controlled the 'licence raj' referred to by Gurcharan Das above) in the state capitals and in New Delhi were essential for success post-1947. Only two constituencies were able to pull this off:

- Giant public sector companies that the successive socialist governments—heavily influenced by the perceived success of communism in the USSR—chose to cultivate and capitalize on (e.g., State Bank of India,

Steel Authority of India, Coal India, Bharat Heavy
Electricals Ltd). Many of these firms had actually
been private-sector entities that the government of
India had nationalized by fiat—e.g., State Bank of
India, Air India and Coal India.
•   Family-run conglomerates that had already attained
scale, wealth and success in the pre-Independence
era—e.g., the Tatas, Birlas, M&M, Godrej and TVS.

For pretty much everybody else, the first three decades after
Independence was a really challenging time.

*Era 2: Socialism Begins to Retreat, the First Signs
of Economic Liberalization (1979–1990)*

After returning to power in the 1979 elections, Prime Minister
Indira Gandhi began relaxing some of the draconian rules
that had constituted the licence raj. The result was a wave
of entrepreneurial activity. At the forefront of this wave was
Reliance Industries, with Dhirubhai Ambani at the helm.
Hamish McDonald's book *Ambani and Sons* (2010) has several
examples of how Reliance navigated the tricky waters of the
licence raj in the 1980s. Here is one:

Indira Gandhi's return to power opened a golden period for
Dhirubhai Ambani. In 1979 he barely made it to the list
of India's fifty biggest companies, measured by annual sales,
profits or assets. By 1984 Reliance was in the largest five.
Dhirubhai himself had become one of the most talked- and
written-about persons in India, gaining a personal following
more like that of a sports or entertainment star than a
businessman. It was also the period when Dhirubhai made
the most rapid part of his transition, in the bitter words of a
senior non-Congress politician in 1996, 'from supplicant –

the most abject kind of supplicant – to influencer and then to controller of Indian politics' . . .

In October 1980 Reliance received one of the three licences given by the government for manufacture of polyester filament yarn, the location being stipulated as the 'backward' area of Patalganga in the hills of Maharashtra, inland from Bombay. In a field of forty-three contestants for the licences, Reliance beat many larger and longer-established business houses, including Birla. Its licensed capacity of 10,000 tonnes a year was by far the largest and, at the time, close to India's entire existing polyester fibre output.

First Indira Gandhi, and then, after her assassination in 1984, her son Rajiv began relaxing some of draconian restrictions which were suffocating the Indian economy. Amongst the changes were:

- Relaxations in External Trade: Throughout the 1980s, the number of goods placed on the open general licence (OGL) list steadily increased, which effectively meant more items could now legally be imported into the country. Apart from this, the 'canalized' imports (or imports that only the government was permitted to do) were reduced, paving the way for private players to step into this space.
- Beginnings of Industrial Deregulation and Tax Reforms: The Maruti 800 was introduced in 1982. After the 1950s, this was the first time a new car was introduced in India. This was emblematic of the slow yet definite reforms that were beginning to take shape in the form of delicensing of industries, permission for industry to switch between similar production lines (like cars and trucks), permission to expand by more than two times if certain utilization levels were hit and the raising of the minimum asset value mentioned under the Monopolies and Restrictive Trade Practices (MRTP) Act, which removed a lot of the

relatively mid-sized companies out of its purview. This, along with the shift from multi-point and increasingly complex excise duties to a value added tax (VAT), further gave manufacturers impetus to set up shop.

- Emergence of a Realistic Exchange Rate: Since India was a closed economy that was heavily regulated and practically run by the sovereign, free-market forces were never allowed to play out. One perverse impact of this was the relative overvaluation of the Indian currency, which stayed elevated until the 1980s and as a result rendered India uncompetitive in the global context. Come 1980, this situation began to correct as the Indian rupee was allowed to depreciate to more realistic levels vis-à-vis the dollar and other currencies.

Why did India's policymakers start opening up the economy to greater private-sector participation in the early 1980s? The answer lies in the situation in the country in the closing years of the 1970s. The Janata government had collapsed in 1979 and Indira Gandhi had returned as the prime minister. During this period, the economy was hammered by major oil shocks on account of wars in the Middle East and a severe domestic drought. As a result, GDP fell by almost 6 per cent in FY 1980, which meant that per capita income fell by more than 8 per cent, leading to widespread anguish.

In a celebrated paper published in 2004, Dani Rodrik and Arvind Subramanian say:

> . . . the trigger for India's economic growth was an attitudinal shift on the part of the national government in 1980 in favor of private business. The rhetoric of the reigning Congress Party until that time had been all about socialism and pro-poor policies. When Indira Gandhi returned to power in 1980, she re-aligned herself politically with the organized private sector and dropped her previous rhetoric. The

national government's attitude towards business went from being outright hostile to supportive. Indira's switch was further reinforced, in a more explicit manner, by Rajiv Gandhi following his rise to power in 1984. This, in our view, was the key change that unleashed the animal spirits of the Indian private sector in the early 1980s . . .

A pro-business orientation, on the other hand, is one that focuses on raising the profitability of the established industrial and commercial establishments. It tends to favor incumbents and producers. Easing restrictions on capacity expansion for incumbents, removing price controls, and reducing corporate taxes (all of which took place during the 1980s) are examples of pro-business policies, while trade liberalization (which did not take place in any significant form until the 1990s) is the archetypal market-oriented policy . . .[3]

The result of this modest opening up was a doubling of the economic growth rate. In fact, the 1980s was the first period of strong economic growth India had seen post-Independence (GDP growth was 5.5 per cent per annum through the 1980s). Economic growth awakened the Indian investor's animal spirits and resulted in a massive stock market boom (the Sensex compounded at an astonishing 22 per cent per annum through the 1980s). Several of our relatives entered the stock market for the first time in this decade, and the pink newspapers started becoming visible in the living rooms of Indian families as the Maruti 800 cars entered their garages.

However, the 1980s boom contained one fatal flaw—India's fiscal deficit rose from 7.5 per cent in 1980 to 9.4 per cent[4] in 1991. As government spending stoked economic growth in the country, imports started rising from the mid-1980s onwards, putting pressure on India's balance of payments. Saddam Hussein's invasion of Kuwait in 1990 sent oil prices soaring, thus pushing up India's imports further, triggering a balance-of-payments crisis in 1991 as the country ran out of foreign exchange. This crisis ushered in a new era for India.

Era 3: End of the 'Licence Raj', Beginning of the Indian Renaissance (1991–2013)

For those of us who lived through the momentous summer of 1991, it was an unforgettable time. In the space of two months, Prime Minister Narasimha Rao and Finance Minister Manmohan Singh used the dire balance-of-payments crisis in the country to leave behind four decades of socialism and open up the Indian economy, both to the private sector and to foreigners. The impact was immediate and electric, as described by the economist Shrayana Bhattacharya in *Desperately Seeking Shah Rukh: India's Lonely Young Women and the Search for Intimacy and Independence* (2021):

> As an uneducated working-class woman, you might have not had the words or jargon to sum up the phenomenon, but you knew something dramatic had happened in the mid '90s; the evidence was everywhere you looked. So, you wove images into a timeline of your own. You told me that your world, quite literally, started to shrink – the forests of Jharkhand, the textile factories of Gujarat, the farm yields of Bengal, the hemlines of Delhi's skirts, the certainty of a man earning a monthly income. Your world expanded too: the government gave more grains; activists, panchayat meetings, new advertising billboards and polio camps dotted the year; roads began to connect every village to the rest of the country. The patwari, effectively the local land registrar, began to wear jeans. Well-meaning women visited every month, saying they were health workers. Your children started receiving meals at the new government school. The local store offered a buffet

of creams and powders, choices one only imagined available to actresses and princesses. Phone booths became ubiquitous. Your call was almost certain to connect. And, as India turned the corner into a new millennium, Shah Rukh's face was plastered everywhere.

Men started to move away from their fields and find jobs in the cities, bringing artefacts and diseases from the modern world as presents. Suddenly, everyone you knew worked on a construction site. The earth smelled of cement and rubber. Royals became hoteliers. You found yourself orphaned from all the familiar routines – everything had a price, farming was no longer an ideal way of life, news from other parts of the world travelled faster than ever before.

After four decades of believing that foreigners would 'drain' India, India's policymakers—under pressure from the IMF and the World Bank—now opened up the country's economy to foreign investors. After four decades of trying to prop up public sector companies to build the Indian economy, the government now allowed the private sector to invest capital across most parts of the economy.

Two distinct types of entrepreneurs emerged over this remarkable twenty-year period:

- Larger-than-life entrepreneurs, like Karsanbhai Patel (Nirma), Dhirubhai Ambani (Reliance), the Ruias (Essar), the Dhoots (Videocon), the Jindals (Jindal Steel) and the Hindujas (Ashok Leyland, IndusInd Bank, Gulf Oil) built pan-India scale and muscle (both financial and political). They were financed primarily by public-sector banks over this period, with the domestic capital markets playing second fiddle. Private-sector banks did not have meaningful financing capacity at this stage of India's economic evolution. Access to polity remained critical for success as licenses, permissions, permits aplenty were still required. However, the new-generation entrepreneurs were able to muscle into the corridors of power that mattered and get relevant access.

• Technocratic entrepreneurs, educated either in India's elite institutes of higher education (the IITs, IIMs, BITS, IISc, NCL) or educated abroad, emerged and scaled up large businesses—e.g., Deepak Parekh (HDFC), Narayana Murthy (Infosys), Ratan Tata (Tata group), Yusuf Hamied (Cipla), Anji Reddy (Dr Reddy's) and Desh Bandhu Gupta (Lupin).

While the old, established elites faced the challenge of holding their grip on the keys to the kingdom of wealth, their way of life (i.e., speaking BBC English, cultivating the ways of the West) was what many other Indians aspired to. Kashyap Deorah's description of his fellow IIT (Mumbai) students' mindset in the closing decade of the previous century describes this yearning—both for India to be seen on parity with the West and for life in the West itself—*The Golden Tap* (2015):

We were blazing the trail for IIT Bombay to become another Stanford University and Powai to become another Silicon Valley. We were building a global company out of India when the only tech business that India was known for was IT services and outsourcing. We had raised equity capital when there were no venture capitalists investing in early-stage tech start-ups in India. We were starting a movement by staying back in India when everyone in our batch left for the US and those who stayed were the ones who could not go . . .

For Indians to see the world on their own terms, rather than seeing everything benchmarked to a Western norm, we needed the onset of a new era.

Era 4: Capitalism, Increasingly Unfettered (2014 to Date)

As the government increasingly withdrew from being a provider of goods and services, India's policymakers became more focused on improving the country's physical and technology infrastructure. The impact of this on the economy was transformational, as this excerpt from Nandan Nilekani and Viral Acharya's book *Rebooting India: Realizing a Billion Aspirations* (2015) shows:

> Seventy-year-old Basudeb Pahan lives in a densely forested, remote area of Jharkhand. In order to receive his old-age pension from the Government of India, Pahan had to journey fifteen kilometers through hills and jungles to reach Ramgarh, the nearest settlement with a bank branch. And this was only half the story. To collect the 400 rupees a month owed to him, Pahan had to spend hours standing in line. Sometimes he needed to come back the next day. Factoring in the cost of travel and food, Pahan was spending 12 per cent of his pension even before he received it. To add to his woes, he often had to wait two to three months for his payment to be processed. Pahan, the local government, and indeed the entire pension disbursement system were stuck in a time warp.
>
> Then, in 2011, Pahan found himself transported from a dusty backwater of history into the forefront of India's technological revolution. He achieved this feat by walking a short distance to the local panchayat office in his village and using a device called a micro ATM, under the supervision of the local business correspondent appointed by a bank.

The micro ATM, a handheld wireless device, required only an active mobile data connection in order to function. The business correspondent entered Pahan's twelve-digit Aadhaar number into the device. Pahan pressed his fingers on an attached fingerprint reader and, seconds later, the business correspondent was handing Pahan his money, just as a bank teller might.

The combination of the government focus on building physical infrastructure and on providing the enabling legislation and institutions for a massive digital build-out has resulted in India becoming a 'networked' economy over the past decade:

- The national highway network saw a near doubling,[5] from ~79,000 km in 2012 to ~140,000 km in 2022; domestic air travel passengers more than trebling,[6] from ~54 mn in 2009 to ~170 mn in 2019 (pre-pandemic); households with broadband connections[7] growing ~seven times, from ~20 mn in 2013 to ~137 mn in 2023; the number of bank accounts growing ~three times, from ~100 crore[8] in 2015 to ~300 crore[9] in 2023.
- The India Stack was built. It began with Aadhaar UIDAI (Unique Identification Authority of India) in 2009, which gave a digital identity to all citizens of the country. This was followed by the introduction of Jan Dhan bank accounts in 2014, which successfully gave every Indian family a bank account. This, combined with the proliferation of mobile phone usage in India and the launch of Jio's ultra-cheap mobile broadband services in 2017, networked India digitally. This in turn paved the way for the creation of the Unified Payments Interface (UPI), where anyone with a bank account and a smartphone with an Internet connection could transfer

any amount of money to anyone in the country instantly! Today, more than 9 billion UPI transactions[10] take place each month, and over half of India's GDP is being transacted via UPI.

- The cost of capital dropped sharply, measured not just by the 10 year-government of India bond yield (which has dropped from ~9 per cent in August 2013 to ~7 per cent currently) but also by the large pools of private equity and venture capital money that now flow into India each year (anywhere between $20 bn and $70bn per annum, depending on what the US Federal Reserve is doing with its monetary policy). Alongside foreign capital, the rapid financialization of savings (e.g., the number of brokerage, or demat, accounts has grown eight times over the past decade) has driven a structural downtrend in the cost of both debt and equity capital.

However, two areas where the country has stayed puzzlingly backward are health and education. As a percentage of GDP, spending by the states and by the Central government went down from 5.2 per cent[11] in FY15[12] to 4.7 per cent[13] in FY23.[14] This, combined with the economic impact of Covid-19, meant that by 2023, items linked with the lower-income sections of the population (e.g., FMCG, two-wheelers, apparel, Hawaii chappals) were showing annual volume growth of barely 2–3 per cent, i.e., broadly the same as India's population growth, implying that on a per capita basis, low-income Indians' ability to purchase the essentials of life was stalling.

Changes in the Indian Economy of the Future

As socialism fades away and the Indian economy moves towards an increasingly unfettered pan-India free market, the gap between the winners and losers will widen along multiple dimensions:

Companies Who Operate Outside the 'Formal' Economy Will Struggle

In an increasingly integrated large economy, SMEs are struggling to compete against the larger, better-capitalized companies. SMEs, who for decades had survived by evading taxes, found it hard to deal with the Exchequer's scrutiny once India moved to a common indirect tax (GST) for the entire country in 2017. As we highlight in the final chapter of the book, 56 per cent of registered Indian companies filing 'non-zero' corporate tax returns have failed to grow their profits in real terms (i.e. after taking inflation into account) over the past decade. Cumulatively, these firms account for just 2 per cent of India Inc's profits. In contrast, the 900 most profitable companies in the country account for 62 per cent of the nation's profits. These highly profitable companies have grown their profits at 15 per cent per annum over the past decade.

Wealth Polarized in Hands of Well-Educated, Well-Connected People

India's GDP has risen from US$ 607 bn[15] in 2003 to US$ 3.75 tn[16] in 2023. This six time jump in national income over a twenty-year period has been unevenly distributed. In a country where the per capita income is Rs 2 lakhs ($2.5K), a tiny elite of around 250,000 Indian families (or 1 roughly million individuals) are reporting annual taxable income in excess of Rs 1 crore (US$ 120K). An article in the Indian Express based on data from the Income Tax Department says:

> Over 2.69 lakh income tax returns were filed for income above Rs 1 crore for the financial year 2022–23, an increase of 49.4 per cent from the pre-pandemic year of 2018–19, while returns filed for income up to Rs 5 lakh rose by 1.4 per cent in the same period, as per e-filing data of the Income

Tax Department. In absolute terms, 2.69 lakh income tax returns were filed for income above Rs 1 crore for financial year 2022–23 as against 1.93 lakh for 2021–22 and 1.80 lakh for 2018–19[17] (emphasis is ours).

Separately, the consulting firm BCG found that in the two decades between 1999 and 2019, the Indian elite's wealth grew 15.8x.

Economic Growth Polarized in Favour of Few Highly Developed States

As we highlight in Chapter 6, thanks to significantly higher levels of education, superior social indicators (in terms of law and order, infant mortality, women's labour-force participation) and superior physical infrastructure, peninsular India now accounts for around a quarter of India's population, half of India's GDP and almost 60 per cent of India's economic growth. Peninsular states like Telangana now boast per capita income levels of Rs 3.2 lakh ($4K), almost 50 per cent higher than the national average, and have seen their per capita income double in the past six to seven years. Almost all of India's private sector capex is going to peninsular India (with Gujarat and the NCR being the only parts of the country outside the peninsula to see significant investments).

While within peninsular India the seven states are increasingly seeing convergence in per capita income (around the Rs 3.2 lakh ($4K) mark), these states are pulling away from the rest of the country—i.e., the northern and eastern states are increasingly falling behind.

Need for Increased Fiscal Transfers

Given that India is a democracy, in order to win elections, parties across the political spectrum will have to transfer money into the bank accounts of voters left behind even while economic growth is sweeping across this vast land. This can be seen in the opening exhibit of this chapter (which shows how government spending as a percentage of GDP has steadily increased) and in the table below (which shows how government spending on education, food, fuel and fertilizers has risen over the past decade).

Table 3.3: Rise in Indian Government Spending as Percentage of GDP

Eras in the Indian Economy	Government Capex as a % of GDP	Government Spending on Healthcare as a % of GDP	Government Spending on Education as a % of GDP	Government Spending on Food, Fertilizer, and Petroleum Subsidies as a % of GDP
Era 1: 1947-1979	4.9%"	NA	NA	NA
Era 2: 1980-1990	6.70%	NA	NA	1.10%
Era 3: 1991-2013	3.80%	0.89%*	3.2%*	1.50%
Era 4: 2014-2024	4.10%	1.10%	3.0%'"	1.7%'

Source: Budgetary documents (sourced from IIFL Capital), RBI; all data for government spending considers both state and central government spending; reliable and continuous data available only after 1971, and therefore the start year considered is 1971—government capex data taken from budget documents and for pre-2008–09 divided by current GDP; data for healthcare and education expenditure by central governments begin from 2009–10; healthcare and education expenditure under both capex and revenue expenditure has been summed and divided by nominal GDP for that year; data for 2023–24 is a Revised Estimate; all years considered are financial years.

The electoral compulsion to spend money could also be seen whenever elections are held. As award-winning journalist and author Shankkar Aiyar wrote when campaigning for the assembly elections of 2023 was underway:

> It is instructive that the contest in the poll bound states is less about ideas and ideology and more a competition of schemes. In state after state, political parties have designed schemes to contain discontentment.
>
> . . . Unlike in the past the schemes are targeted to harvest votes—based on parameters of caste, class and gender.

Women voters—who constitute 78 million of the 161.4 million voters[18]—are deemed the X factor, game changer. The instrument of endearment is direct cash benefit transfer. In Madhya Pradesh the Shivraj Chauhan regime has promised to up the cash transfer under the Ladli Behna[19] scheme from Rs 1250 to Rs 1500 and raise it to Rs 3000 per month.

. . . There is the promise of direct cash transfer and then there is the top-up strategy where states add to the payments/subsidies provided by the Centre with additional allocations from the state kitty.

. . . Cash benefit transfers and top ups for subsidies have been enabled by the availability of the Aadhaar-based DBT-Bharat[20]. Indeed state governments have registered over 7500 user codes[21] for a plethora of transfers on the NPCI grid. For sure there is no free lunch but political parties are not obliged to outline the costs of the promises or how the additional expenditure will be funded . . . [22]

Foreign Capital Flooding In

Foreign investors have invested roughly $3.5 trillion[23] in the Chinese stock market, which has registered a total CAGR return (in US$) of 4.5 per cent over the past decade (source: Bloomberg). In contrast, foreign investors have invested $0.6 trillion[24] in the Indian stock market, which has registered a total CAGR return (in US$) of 10.1 per cent over the past decade (source: Bloomberg)—i.e., more than two times the return generated by the Chinese market. If you stretch this data back to twenty years or thirty years, the conclusion remains broadly the same. The only large stock market in the world that has been able to keep up with India over the past thirty years is that of the USA. With rising concerns around the Chinese economy and geopolitics, Western allocators have turned their attention to India as an alternative market in which to invest capital.

A similar story seems likely to play out on the FDI front. Over the past decade, foreign investors have on average pumped around US$ 120 bn[25] per annum into China, against only US$ 12 bn[26] per annum into India. With the Chinese and American governments now at loggerheads, these FDI inflows into China have stopped altogether. With America keen to use India as a counterweight to China, it is likely that some of these flows will come into India. We will return to this subject in Chapter 7.

India needs both FPI and FDI flows to finance its current account deficit, which oscillates between 2 per cent and 3 per cent of GDP ($60–$100 bn per annum) as India's domestic financial savings hit a 50-year low.[27]

Unlike the east Asian economies (which grew by exporting goods made by low-wage workers), India's growth is fuelled by a large services economy (55 per cent of GDP) and by the export of knowledge-intensive services (IT services exports amount to $250 bn per annum) and products (pharma exports amount to $25 bn per annum).[28] Remittances from Indians living abroad bring in more than $100 bn of inflows.[29] Therefore, with around $400 bn per annum (9 per cent of GDP) coming into India every year, thanks to the intellectual horsepower of India's well-educated middle class, the INR tends to be an overvalued currency. This makes it almost impossible for India to be an exporter of low-end manufactured goods like clothes, shoes and sports goods. The overvalued Indian rupee also makes imported goods (especially electronic items, overseas holidays and overseas education) relatively cheap for Indians, thus fuelling the current account deficit and a low domestic financial savings rate.[30] To square this circle, India needs to continue to attract foreign capital. Given the disappointing experience foreign investors have had in China, even if 10 per cent of the amounts they have invested in China over the past decade wings its way to India, the impact on the Indian economy will be transformational.

Summary

Post-1947, India's economy has been through four distinct eras. Now, with socialism fading away and with the country increasingly operating as a free-market economy, we see five distinct directions in which India's economy will evolve over the next decade:

1. SMEs will continue to struggle to compete against well managed, efficient, tech savvy sector leading franchises;
2. Wealth will polarize in the hands of well-educated and well-connected businesspeople;
3. Economic growth will polarize in favour of a few highly developed states;
4. Fiscal transfers will have to increase to mitigate the polarizing effects of the preceding developments; and
5. Foreign capital will flood into India.

Section 2

Themes of Change

4

The Rise of Indian Women

'India Today News Desk
Maharajganj, UPDATED: Jul 10, 2024 17:13 IST
Edited By: Vadapalli Nithin Kumar (With inputs from
Amitesh Tripathi)

Around eleven married women have gone missing from different villages in Uttar Pradesh's Maharajganj district after receiving the first instalment of the PM Awas Gramin Yojana. One of them has allegedly eloped with her lover.

The government scheme provides financial assistance to poor and middle-class families in building a permanent home.

The issue came to light after a man, Sanjay, reported that his wife, Suniya, was missing after she received the first tranche of Rs 40,000 of the scheme.

Preliminary investigation by the Block Development Officer revealed that Suniya had eloped with an unknown person, taking the Rs 40,000 installment recently released by the government. . .

Subsequently, 10 other similar cases came to light, where husbands reported their wives to be missing.

Suniya's father-in-law requested the government to transfer the remaining two instalments to his son Sanjay's account.

> 'The money was sent to our daughter-in-law's account, and we later found out she had run away with a boy. We demand the government send the money to my son's account,' he said. . .
>
> However, this is not the first such incident. Previously, four women from Barabanki district ran away with their lovers on receiving Rs 50,000 as part of the scheme.'[1]

The Rise of an Entrepreneur from Jail Road Market, Delhi

Nestled in the crowded bazaar of Jail Road Market in New Delhi is a tiny shop selling colourful kurtas and pants for women, a common business in this neighborhood and in hundreds of similar markets across northern India. However, the owner of this shop and her story are anything but common. The owner is Jasmeen Kaur, creator of the now famous words 'So beautiful, so elegant, just looking like a wow!'

Kaur shot to fame with this catchy phrase when Bollywood star Deepika Padukone recited it on social media and made it famous. The rise of Instagram and social media, as well as their accessibility to millions of Indians, ensured that the phrase 'looking like a wow' became 'viral' and made Kaur a celebrity, potentially creating a pan-India—as opposed to local—market for her wares. She signifies the rise of a new India; an India where polished English and high-profile university degrees and MBAs are no longer a prerequisite for success.

Exhibit 4.1: Jasmeen Kaur, the Lady Who Started the Viral Trend of 'Just Looking Like a Wow'

Source: Instagram (sourced from India TV); images used only for illustration purposes, their copyrights remain with their respective creators

Today India has millions of successful women entrepreneurs like Kaur. According to Bain and Co, there are approximately 15.7 million women-run enterprises in India, constituting 22 percent of the overall entrepreneurial landscape, a figure that has the potential to rise to 30 million with further support and encouragement.[2] For example, 500 km from Mumbai, in the buzzing industrial town of Dewas in Madhya Pradesh (with a population of approximately 2 mn),[3] a mother earns a livelihood by making and selling papads on Meesho, an online marketplace for consumer goods, especially popular in tier-3 and tier-4 cities. The profits she generates from selling this humble Indian snack enables her to not only pay for her daily expenses but also for her son's tuitions, thus making her financially independent of the men in her family.[4]

Rather than being exceptions, such stories are the norm today in India. Women throughout the country are successfully launching their own businesses. According to Periodic Labour Force Survey (PLFS) data, women's share in self-employment has been steadily rising in India, especially in rural areas, whereas men's share in self-employment has been falling (see exhibit below).

Exhibit 4.2: Rising Percentage of Women among Self-Employed

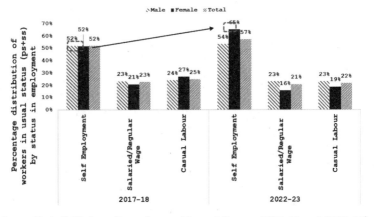

Source: Periodic Labour Force Survey (Annual Report 2022–23 and 2017–18); the period under consideration is July 2017–June 2018 and July 2022–June 2023, respectively; data taken for rural+urban

While the self-employed category is vast and includes unpaid labour too, if we go one level deeper and see the stratification within the self-employed, the rise of women entrepreneurs (rather than 'woman unpaid' labour) is evident. In the exhibit below, for women, the share of 'self-employment by own account' (i.e. running an enterprise of one's own) and 'self-employment as an employer' (i.e. running a business in which the owner is an employee and, in addition, employs others) has increased between 2017–18 (when PLFS started) and 2022–23. It is notable, that the same trends are *not* visible for male workers. Even more remarkably, the share of women performing unpaid labour has gone down during this time period.

Exhibit 4.3: Sharp Rise in Employer Sub-Category for
Self-Employed Women

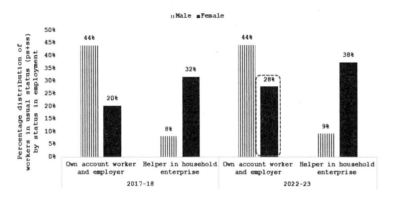

Source: Periodic Labour Force Survey (Annual Report 2022–23 and 2017–18); period under consideration is July 2017–June 2018 & July 2022–June 2023, respectively; data taken for rural+urban

So, what is going on here? What are the drivers of the rapid rise in entrepreneurship among Indian women? We believe there are several forces at work here, including rising education levels among women, greater access to financing for women and greater female political participation.

Surging Education Levels Game Changer for Women

While education has not changed the male engineer's mind, education has empowered this girl to walk out of a marriage and earn her own livelihood and to bring up her daughter. Such economic independence would not have been possible without education. I saw this again and again as I travelled through different parts of the country. It was heartening to see in Census 2011, for the first time, the number of additional literate women in the last ten years exceeding

the number of additional literate men. This convergence
of literacy rates over the next ten years will be a big driver
of women's economic independence and empowerment
in my view.

—Anirudha Dutta, author of *Half a Billion Rising:*
The Emergence of Indian Women (2015)[5]

When, a decade ago, Anirudha Dutta was researching his
prescient book on the rise of Indian women, the women in
question were just nudging ahead of India's men in the gender
parity index (GPI), which measures the number of girls per
boys getting enrolled in school, across all levels of the education
system (primary, secondary and higher secondary).

Exhibit 4.4: GPI Greater than 1.00 GPI Due to Rise in Female
Enrollment in Schools

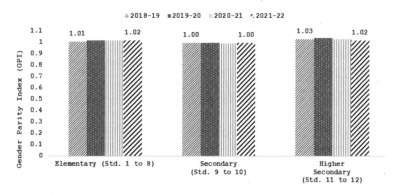

Source: Department of School Education and Literacy, Ministry of Education;
GPI refers to the gross enrolment ratio of girls divided by gross enrolment ratio
of boys at different levels of education and measures how many girls per boy are
getting enrolled in schools in a given school year

In fact, if we go one step further and look at the GPI for higher
education (i.e., for the age group of eighteen to twenty-three years),
not only is the GPI greater than one across all social categories

(see exhibit below), but the improvement has also been most rapid among women from the scheduled castes and scheduled tribes, indicating that women from the most disadvantaged sections of Indian society are powering ahead the fastest.

Exhibit 4.5: Caste Agnostic Trend of More Women Being Educated for Longer

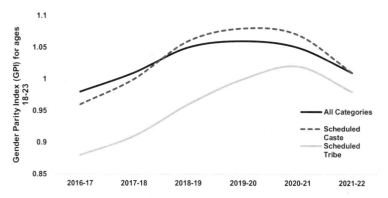

Source: All India Survey on Higher Education, Department of Higher Education, Government of India; Gender parity index refers to the gross enrolment ratio of girls divided by gross enrolment ratio of boys at different levels of education and measures how many girls per boy are getting enrolled in institutes of higher education in a given academic year

Not only are more Indian women getting educated, but they are also getting educated more rapidly than their male counterparts. India's female literacy rate in 2011 was 64.6 per cent, and the male literacy rate 80.6 per cent. However, between 1961 and 2011, female literacy in India has grown three times faster than male literacy (approximately 3 per cent per annum, vis-à-vis approximately 1 per cent per annum).[6]

However, the ascendancy of Indian women in education is even more comprehensive than what the enrolment numbers suggest; not only are more women getting educated than men, but the women are also getting better educated than men.

We know this because in May 2023, the pass percentage of girls was 6 percentage points higher than that of boys[7] in the class twelve examinations of the Central Board of Secondary Education (CBSE).

Education: Major Driver of Delayed Workforce Entry

Interestingly though, despite the uptrend in the educational attainment of women in the country, their labour force participation rate (LFPR) has been trending down since 2000, when it peaked at around 31 per cent (see exhibit below). And while the rate has improved significantly post-Covid, it remains low relative to other countries at a similar stage of development.

Exhibit 4.6: Female LFPR had Trending Down for Twenty Years

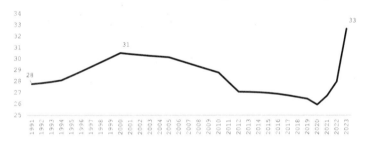

Source: ILO-modelled estimates from World Bank; Labour force participation rate is the proportion of the population aged fifteen and older that is economically active; calendar years used here.

Given this seemingly worrying trend in the data, there is naturally a lot of concern around both the employability and income of Indian women. Are these concerns justified, and is the situation of Indian women really worse than what it was thirty years ago?

We believe the answer to both these questions is an emphatic 'no'. Indian women today are in a much better position, socially and financially, than they ever were. There are primarily three reasons why we believe so.

When someone stays longer in the education system, their entry into the workforce will be later than it would have been had they not studied for longer. If we look at the LFPR data, but with a different lens, namely age-wise stratification, a completely new picture emerges. While the LFPR for women in the age bracket of 15–24 has gone down substantially since 2010, the LFPR for the age bracket of 25–35 has remained fairly stable; and, remarkably, the LFPR for the 35-plus age bracket has actually gone up (see exhibit below).

Exhibit 4.7: Share of Women Aged 15–24 Falls in LFPR, Due to More Years Spent in Education

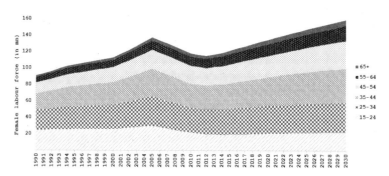

Source: ILO-modelled estimates, Our World in Data; underlying database created as of 2017, and therefore all the figures 2018 onwards are estimates; all figures in million; data as of calendar years

Combining this with the fact that a majority of India's demography in the past decade was in the 15–24 age bracket[8], it implies that as more girls were getting educated, the LFPR was impacted adversely. However, such an impact is optical, because as this cohort starts entering the workforce, the LFPR will improve. Ironically, if you believe in this line of thought, a more decisive improvement in LFPR will only happen when India starts to age (because then, in proportional terms, fewer Indian women will be entering higher education, and a greater proportion will be in the workforce).

Greater Access to 'Financing' For Women

Financialization of the Indian economy has transformed how Indians deal with their monies and their investments. As a result of Jan Dhan and UPI, more women today hold bank accounts vis-à-vis their male counterparts. According to World Bank data, the proportion of women above fifteen years of age holding any financial account divided by the proportion of men above fifteen years of age holding a financial account crossed the ratio of 1 in 2021 itself, meaning that a greater proportion of women is in the financial system today (as a percentage of total women) than their male counterparts in the financial system as a percentage of total men.

Exhibit 4.8: Proportion of Women with Bank Accounts Surpasses that of Men

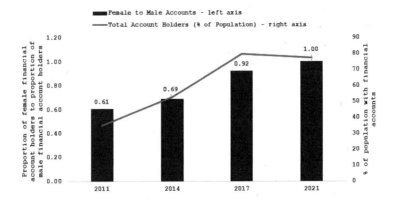

Source: World Bank gender data portal, 2021; proportion of females owning financial accounts (out of all women) is divided by the proportion of men owning financial accounts (out of all men); financial account means an account with any type of a financial institution or a mobile-money-service provider (of people over fifteen years of age) in a calendar year.

As more women are included in the financial system, they are finding it easier to get access to credit. That, in turn, means business expansion has become much easier than before (courtesy their bank statements containing hundreds of UPI transactions, which validate the revenues being generated by their enterprises).

Furthermore, a study conducted by MassChallenge and BCG for multiple countries[9] found that startups founded or co-founded by women got less funding but generated more revenues than those founded or co-founded solely by men (see exhibit below). This implies that women are better capital allocators than men.

Exhibit 4.9: Women are Better Capital Allocators on Average, Despite Receiving Less Funding

Source: BCG article on Diversity, Equity, and Inclusion ('Why Women-Owned Startups are a Better Bet', 2018)

Basis the debt default (gross non-performing assets, or GNPA) data, women are better borrowers (see exhibit below). From a lender's perspective, women entrepreneurs are the perfect conduit through which a lender can lock into the flywheel of higher credit, resulting in greater investments into business, greater revenues and profits, and therefore greater payback of credit and lower delinquencies, leading to higher credit uptake again.

Exhibit 4.10: Indian Women Better Borrowers than Indian Men

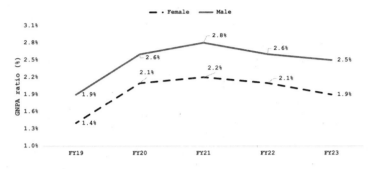

Source: CRIF Highmark, CRISIL MI&A (sourced from CRISIL's Industry Report on Housing Finance Market in India, August 2023)

Urban India: Women Have More Money in Bank Accounts than Men

The flow of money into bank accounts is a function of the account owner's earnings. At a pan-India level, as of 2023, men on average hold approximately Rs 90,000 in their bank accounts, whereas women hold less than half that amount.[10]

However, the numbers change dramatically if we look at the bank deposits data for urban India, where the role of physical strength in earning money is lower than it is in rural India. In 'urban' areas (defined by the RBI as centres with a population of above 1 lakh but less than 10 lakh), in 2023, for the first time in Indian history, women's deposit balances exceeded those of men (see exhibit below where 1 reflects parity between the deposits of men and women and a figure higher than 1 indicates that women have higher deposits than men). More stunningly, in 'metropolitan' areas (defined by the RBI as areas with population greater than 10 lakh), women's average deposit ticket size has grown by 10 per cent from 2019 to 2023 and are now significantly higher than those of men!

Exhibit 4.11: On Average, Metro and Urban Area Women Hold
More Money in Deposits than Men

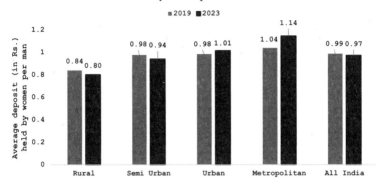

Source: National Statistics Office, MOSPI; metric used is average deposit or total deposit for men and women each divided by the number of accounts held by each gender, disaggregated by geography

In the years to come, as the Indian economy moves increasingly from domination by industries investing in tangible assets to industries investing in intangible assets, the kind of jobs that incrementally get generated will require greater intellectual muscle than physical strength. With better-skilled women entering the workforce, wherever the demand for skilled labour gets satisfied by this cohort, there is every reason to believe that wealth and income will swing in favour of urban India's women even more decisively.[11]

While the chart above suggests that it is only in recent years that urban Indian women's bank accounts have become bigger than their male counterparts', we believe that there is a high probability that this trend goes back at least a decade. However, until the rise of Jan Dhan and then UPI, many urban women did not have bank accounts of their own, which meant that their money was sitting either at home or in their husbands' bank accounts. Over the last four years, with UPI having become the preferred mode of payment in urban India, Indian women's earning power is showing up not just in their bank accounts but also in how they invest. With the growing ease of access to smartphones, and thanks to low-cost broadband Internet connectivity, Indian women are accessing the financial system not only through bank accounts and traditional instruments like fixed deposits (FDs) but are also experimenting with new-age investment avenues like cryptocurrency. Shaili Chopra writes in her book *Sisterhood Economy* (2017):

> This is a story of a woman who wanted to dabble in cryptocurrency in the words of Kavita Gupta of Delta Blockchain Fund . . . A student from a village in Punjab studying engineering and working as a receptionist had crypto money. She invested Rs 100 every day in crypto from the salary that she earned as a receptionist. Later she earned so much money through crypto that she was able to pay her education loan. So as far as digitalization of financial services are concerned, options for investments and savings have dimensionally increased and become easier and young girls are willingly experimenting.

Narrowing Wage Gap Between Men and Women

While gender parity in wages is an ongoing battle the world over, considerable progress has been made in the last thirty-odd years. According to the International Labour Organization (ILO) and the National Statistical Survey Office (NSSO),[12] India's women on average earned 48 per cent less than their male counterparts in 1993–94. In contrast, in 2018–19, this gap had reduced to 28 per cent. In fact, the Periodic Labour Force Survey (PLFS) for 2021–22,[13] shows that the share of urban women among the regular-wage/salaried employees exceeded that of urban men, at 50.30 per cent. The same cannot be said for rural women and men. Intuitively, this makes sense, as the more educated and skilled women become, the more that jobs requiring intellectual skills will be lapped up by them. Because urban centres provide more such employment opportunities than rural areas, logically that's where women are more likely to excel professionally, and that is precisely what is happening.

Taking this argument to its logical conclusion would suggest that in the most hi-tech part of the Indian economy, women should be earning more than men. That's exactly what surveys of India's tech sector show—women in technology earn on average 7 per cent more than men.[14]

Access to Seed Capital via Government's Direct Transfers

Both the Central and state governments have floated multiple schemes targeted at women, especially before elections, given that women voter turnout has been trending up over the last few election cycles. Worthy of mention amongst them are the schemes that directly transfer hard cash into the bank accounts of women (courtesy Jan Dhan) via direct benefit transfer (DBT).

Schemes like the Pradhan Mantri Matru Vandana Yojana, which transfers Rs 5000 (split into three installments of Rs 1670 each) into the bank accounts of all pregnant and lactating mothers; the Laadli Behna scheme in Madhya Pradesh awarding each woman from 23–60 years of age Rs 1000 per month in their Aadhaar-linked bank accounts, the Lakhpati Didi scheme in Rajasthan, which provides interest-free loans of up to Rs 5 lakh to women to start their own business to earn a steady income; the Karnataka government's Gruha Lakshmi scheme, which provides financial assistance of up to Rs 2000 per month to women from impoverished backgrounds and who are heads of their families, etc., are testament to governments across India's states taking the rising trend of women voters seriously.

Greater Access to Market for Women

India's methodical building of the basic pillars required to undergird a modern economy started in 2009, when Nandan Nilekani, then CEO at Infosys, left his corner office in Bengaluru to work with the government of India undertaking, the Unique Identification Authority of India (UIDAI), to first envision and then implement the herculean task of providing 1.21 billion Indians with a social security-like number, or Aadhaar.

Not only did Aadhaar succeed (there are nearly 1.31 bn[15] unique Aadhaar IDs today in India), but Nilekani's successful demonstration of the concept of social infrastructure also opened the doors for mass financialization, i.e., opening of a bank account for each Indian via the Jan Dhan scheme. In 2022, India had 3 bn[16] bank accounts, up three times from 1.1bn[17] in 2015.

The introduction of low-cost and fast cellular Internet in 2016, courtesy Jio, coupled with widespread smartphone penetration, meant that every Indian now had a legal identity (via Aadhaar), an economic identity (via a Jan Dhan bank account) and a digital identity (via smartphones and the Internet—see the exhibit below to understand the sheer extent of Internet access in India). This trinity of Jan Dhan, Aadhaar and mobile phone usage was soon dubbed as 'JAM'.

Exhibit 4.12: Almost Half of India's Population has Access to Internet

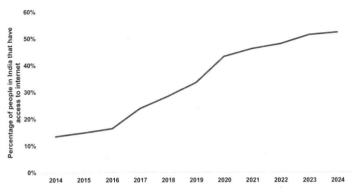

Source: Statista; the figure indicates % of population that has access to any kind of Internet connection (cellular/broadband etc.)

While the JAM trinity has enabled millions of Indians to lead better lives, women in particular have leveraged JAM very effectively to generate income. How so?

- Via their bank accounts, Indians now have access to the Unified Payments Interface (UPI), which facilitates instant bank-to-bank money transfer (without any use of paper). UPI thus helps SMEs pay their suppliers and get paid by their customers instantaneously, and with zero transaction costs.

- Given that Aadhaar numbers give Indians a valid proof of residence and proof of their overall existence, Aadhaar eases the process for SMEs to get regulatory permits and licenses.

- Access to smartphones and cheap broadband (at one fortieth the cost prevalent in the USA), helps Indian SMEs reach out to customers not just in their neighbourhood but also across the land via social media platforms like Instagram and YouTube, thus increasing their total addressable market multifold.

This powerful combination of policy changes, plus tech innovation, has given the new Indian woman entrepreneur access to the 'market'—both the market from which she buys her 'inputs' and the end market in which she sells her wares.

Growing Addressable Market of Women, by Women, for Women

The category of women as buyers is also burgeoning, thanks to digitization and greater access to markets (the same factors that are allowing women to become successful entrepreneurs). But arguably the greatest enabler that has underpinned this revolution, where women are taking control of their financial situation via the self-employment route, is their higher level of education.

Because of this twin benefit of 'access' (to the market and to financing) and knowledge of what to do with that access (courtesy better education), women today have greater financial freedom to embark on an income-generation and consumption journey of their choice. In essence, these changes have enabled for women the opportunity to decide what they wish to do, especially from the comfort of their homes—an option that didn't exist even a decade ago.

India's women entrepreneurs are best suited to cater to the needs of India's women customers because they understand the pain points of this demography better than anyone else. A case in point is the emergence of multi-billion dollar companies like Nykaa (promoter: Falguni Nayar), Mama Earth (promoter: Ghazal Alagh) and Sugar (promoter: Vineeta Singh), who have taken the beauty and personal care market by storm. From a standing start in 2012, Nykaa's revenue share of the total beauty and personal care online market stood at around 27 per cent[18] in 2022.

Historically Most Discriminated Communities Capture Newer, More Rewarding Opportunities

> Negotiating between American and Jewish identities, they operated with a sense of empowerment. They did not believe that they had to accept America as it was, nor did they see Judaism as a fixed entity that they could not mold to fit their needs. They could put their impress on both to ease the traumas of accommodation and to bring the two into harmony.
>
> —Hasia R. Diner, professor of American Jewish History at New York University.[19]

A community that has for centuries faced discrimination in the Western world—thanks to the prevalence of anti-semitism, which goes back a couple of millennia—are the Jews. In that context, the rise of the Jews in America to the point where they dominate the commanding heights of American capitalism is a testament to the fact that in a free-market economy, once a community has access to financing and to the 'market', it should be able to rise. If American Jews are Exhibit #1 of this phenomenon, India's women are on their way to becoming Exhibit #2.

Greater Political Power for Women

> The right to equality in voting is a basic human right in liberal democracy. Women enjoy this right to equality in voting, and by casting a vote, they make a formal expression of their individual choice of political parties, representatives or of broad policies. The fact that more women are voluntarily exercising their constitutional right of adult suffrage across all states in India is testimony to the rise of self-empowerment

of women to secure their fundamental right to freedom of expression. This is an extraordinary achievement in the world's largest democracy with 717 million voters of which 342 million voters are women.

—Dr Shamika Ravi[20]

Kondagaon district, with a population of roughly 43,000[21] in Chhattisgarh State, is often in the news for Naxal uprisings and political turmoil. In this district, which is home to some of the most disadvantaged people in Indian society, resides Lata Usendi, a powerful woman with immense resolve. A seasoned politician, who also served as minister of women and child development in Chhattisgarh previously, Usendi has been actively involved in politics since 1998. While she faced a setback in the 2018 state assembly elections, losing to her rival, she continued working for the betterment of people in the area. As a result, she contested the state assembly election from the same constituency again in 2023 and was elected. The grit and determination demonstrated by Usendi, her passion towards her profession and her aspirations, despite the challenging circumstances, especially in the region that she comes from, is increasingly becoming the norm today in India.

Despite India implementing universal adult franchise (one vote per person, regardless of their caste, creed, gender, etc.) in 1947, the political representation of women in the Indian Parliament has been very low. The number of women getting elected to the lower house of Parliament (or the Lok Sabha) has grown at a meagre 2 per cent CAGR over the last twenty years. Even though rising numbers of women are contesting elections, the percentage of women who get elected to Parliament has gone down materially over the past fifty years. The share of women across elected representatives in the Lok Sabha has risen from 9 per cent to just 14 per cent during the same time period (see exhibit below). What this essentially indicates is that a higher number of women contesting in elections is not translating into a significantly higher number of women getting elected in India.

Exhibit 4.13: Insignificant Political Representation of Indian Women in Parliament

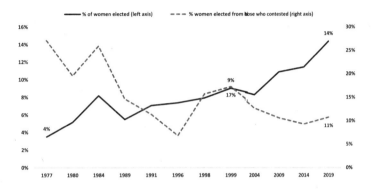

Source: Election Commission of India; complete data is available only for election years post 1977 for these metrics

More Indian Women are Turning Out to Vote

Interestingly, even as women's representation as elected members of Parliament has not improved, more women today than at any point in India's history are exercising their right to vote. If we were to look at the Lok Sabha elections throughout independent India's history, women voters as a percentage of all women registered to vote reached its highest-ever tally in 2019 (in the previous Lok Sabha election). What is even more remarkable is that this ratio for women has already surpassed its equivalent for men in the country; more women than men are exercising their right to vote, with the gender gap ratio turning negative for the first time in 2019 (see exhibit below).

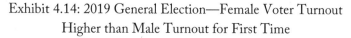

Exhibit 4.14: 2019 General Election—Female Voter Turnout
Higher than Male Turnout for First Time

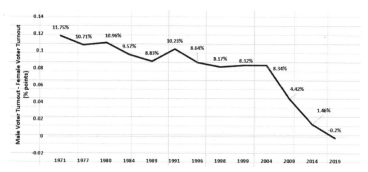

Source: Election Commission of India; complete data was available only after 1971
for this metric; years pertain to the calendar years of general election in India

This dichotomy between lower representation of women
in politics yet greater participation by them in the political
discourse over the years naturally raises two questions: a) why
have women start voting more than before, and b) what are its
implications for the country going forward?

*More Free Time for Women to Engage in
Activities of Choice*

> With the creation of scheduled part-time work in the 1940s
> and its enormous diffusion in the 1950s, the substitution
> effect became larger. Reinforcing factors include the
> almost complete diffusion of modern, electric household
> technologies, such as the refrigerator and the washing
> machine, and the previous diffusion of basic facilities such as
> electricity, running water, and the flush toilet.
>
> —Nobel Laureate Claudia Goldin in the
> Richard T. Ely lecture (2006)[22]

In the United States, during the period 1920–40, thanks to the widespread diffusion of newly invented appliances that ran on electricity (a new innovation by itself at that time), household chores that took all day earlier now took only a fraction of the time. Women, who were at the time the primary agents responsible for running their households, saw their physical strain and effort from managing these activities go down materially, leaving them with spare time to pursue other interests. And so emerged the working class American woman who preferred to engage in part-time work outside the household to earn wages. This is remarkable, as Claudia Goldin has explained, because in the years prior to this period, while some women were engaged in work, the 'income effect' (i.e., the pressing need to earn more money) was the dominant reason why they would engage thus. In other words, they worked out of necessity. The period 1920–40 was the first time when women could choose to work, not out of necessity to sustain the household but because they wished to, shrinking the income effect and increasing the 'substitution effect' (the effect that signifies women working and earning rather than merely supporting the incomes earned by men).

India today appears to be at a similar stage of development as the America of 1920s–40s. Most women in India spent most of their time on household chores, akin to their American counterparts from before the 1920s. This largely involves fetching water from distant sources, washing clothes manually, cooking with firewood and cleaning the house manually—all time-consuming and laborious tasks. Thankfully, recent policy changes have changed the lives of Indian women for the better.

By 2018, the Census recorded that villages in all the states had reported 100 per cent electrification.[23] Secondly, under the Pradhan Mantri Ujjwala Yojana (PMUY), roughly 80 million LPG connections were provided to below-poverty-line households by 2019, thus increasing the total LPG connections from around 140 million in 2014 to more than 320 million as of March 2023.[24]

Thirdly, under the Nal se Jal mission, roughly 145 million rural households (out of the 190 million rural households in the country) have received tap water as of February 2024, up from 30 million in 2019.[25]

These three changes alone have freed up a significant portion of Indian women's time (earlier spent on fetching water from faraway places, washing, cleaning and cooking). The freed-up time can now be used by women for more economically rewarding tasks.

Positive Feedback Loop Between Pro-Women Policy Intervention and Greater Political Participation

The beauty of the government's schemes and policies at the grassroots level lies in a) their being fairly easy to track; and b) their being understood by the intended beneficiaries better because of their improved education and awareness. As the three levers—access to information, more free time to engage in financially rewarding activities and access to capital—have started firing into tangible and measurable benefits for women, they in turn have started applauding the underlying policy changes and are more likely to come out and vote to let this change continue. This seems likely to result in an even higher voter turnout among women in elections in the years to come. That would, in turn, spur policymakers to deliver more benefits to their largest and fastest-growing supporter base. Thus, a positive feedback loop is likely to emerge, which not only materially improves the quality of life of India's women but also brings into the Indian economy highly motivated and enterprising female entrepreneurs.

Summary

For a decade or so now, more women in India are increasingly getting educated (in terms of numbers) and doing it better (in terms of quality) than India's men. Across all levels of the education system, Indian women are outnumbering and outperforming Indian men. Furthermore, data from the RBI shows that women in India's urban areas have more money in their bank accounts than men. Both during our travels and through our number crunching, we can see that urban women are getting wealthier. Entrepreneurship is spreading far faster amongst Indian women than among their male counterparts. And, among registered Indian voters, more women today are voting than men, thanks to greater access to information and business opportunities, and greater availability of free time, facilitated in part by positive policy changes. The key reasons for these advancements appear to be greater access to the end consumer (via the Internet), easier access to financing (courtesy financialization and the India Stack) and a growing target market of aspirational and affluent women

5

The Rise of a New, Educated Elite

... India was, in the simplest way, on the move, that all over the vast country men and women had moved out of the cramped ways and expectations of their parents and grandparents and were expecting more.

—V.S. Naipaul in *India: A Million Mutinies Now* (1989)

Introduction

The networking of India is a very visible spectacle. With individuals having access to Internet surging by about four times, from 14 per cent in 2014 to 52 per cent in 2024,[1] and with bank credit to SMEs (see exhibit below) rising, owing to a rise in the number of bank accounts under Jan Dhan, the last decade has seen a dramatic improvement in India's physical and digital infrastructure.

Exhibit 5.1: Rapid Rise in Internet Penetration Enables Surge in Bank Credit

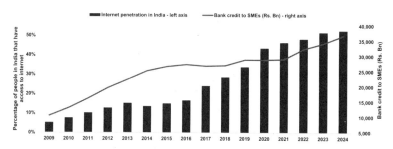

Source: RBI, Statista; bank credit data for 2024 up to 23 February 2024; each year for bank credit is the respective financial year end; Internet penetration data taken up to February 2024; the figures indicated by blue bars show % of population that has access to any kind of Internet connection (cellular/broadband, etc.)

This integration of the Indian economy is altering the composition of the Indian elite by creating opportunity and prosperity for hitherto disadvantaged end economically marginalized groups. How so? you might ask. As journalist Shekhar Gupta explained in The Print: [2]

> As long as the economy was small and growing slowly, the few privileged institutions sufficed to produce the talent India needed, from corporate boardrooms to the civil services and the judiciary. Now, a rapidly growing economy needed many more talented people and a much larger catchment area. St Stephen's/Doon/Mayo/St Columba's/St Xavier's/ La Martinière . . . are still great institutions—they may be India's finest even now—but they are just too few to meet India's need for talent.
>
> That's why a Tata Administrative Services equivalent today needs to go way beyond these institutions, family networks and checking the names of the candidates' fathers.

The desperate, slog 24×7 push of middle, lower middle and poor India, meanwhile, has made it much, much more competitive to crack the UPSC examinations. Track the lists of toppers and rank-holders published by IAS academies when you open our full front pages now, and check if there are any from these old institutions. It is just too hard to compete, and even in the interview process, there is no premium on pedigree.

Exhibit 5.2: 70-Year Uptrend in India's GDP Growth

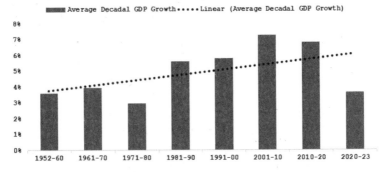

Source: Bloomberg; real GDP growth used here; for the decadal growth in 1960 (the decade that went by), the starting point used is 1952; all years refer to calendar year ends (whose average over decades have been calculated); last observation consists of three years

So, who are the new elites in India? And what are the investment implications of their economic ascent?

Three Sets of New Elites Who Have Risen to Prominence in the Country

As a result of the country getting networked and joined up by means of the physical and digital infrastructure that has been created, economic opportunities that were available only to the elites in the megacities have now became more widely available.

As Nandan Nilekani, the original architect of Aadhaar, has explained:

- Indians who didn't hitherto have any officially verifiable identity got a valid and digitally verifiable identity in the form of Aadhaar.
- Indians who did not have access to information and knowledge now got all the information and knowledge they needed courtesy Jio's low-cost data connections (at one-fortieth of what American telecom companies charge for mobile data).
- Indians who hitherto lacked access to financing from the banking system (and thus had to borrow in the black market at usurious rates) now got access to affordable financing via Jan Dhan bank accounts.

This trifecta of changes made identity, knowledge and financing available to hundreds of millions of Indians who had been living lives of quiet desperation outside the enclaves inhabited by the big-city elites.

Rise of the Non-Elite Educated Entrepreneurs and Executives

Kunal Shah, an angel investor, entrepreneur and founder of fintech company CRED and Freecharge, had to resort to working odd jobs like delivery agent and data entry operator due to his family's bankruptcy. This was revealed by Sanjeev Bikhchandani on social media platform X after meeting Kunal Shah at a coffee shop in Delhi. Bikhchandani recounted meeting Shah at a Delhi coffee shop and learning about his unconventional background. Shah, a philosophy graduate from Wilson College in Mumbai, explained that he chose philosophy because its classes fit his work schedule, not out of personal interest or academic constraints . . .

In a world of IIT IIM Founders he stands out as a
philosophy graduate from Wilson College in Mumbai,
Bikhchandani said in a post.
        The Economic Times, 7 Feb 2024.[3]

Exhibit 5.3: Majority of Promoters and Executive Directors of Nifty50 Companies are Regular Graduates

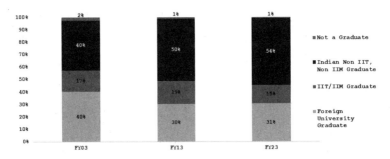

Source: Company annual reports, Bloomberg; non-overlapping promoters and
executive directors for FY03 identified using company annual reports; for FY13
and FY23 Bloomberg was used; Nifty 50 companies as of the respective financial
years were used to build the list of promoters and executive directors; instances
where the educational qualification data was not available were excluded from the
analysis; totals may not seem to be 100 per cent due to rounding

For the first time in the last twenty years, a majority of the
promoters and executive directors of the Nifty 50 companies
are neither from an IIT/IIM nor graduates from any foreign
university. This is remarkable, because twenty years ago, in
FY03, this figure was just 40 per cent, rising to 50 per cent in
FY13. What this graphic and data show is that the majority
of the largest fifty companies in the country today are run by
people who studied in non-elite educational institutions. This
is a natural outcome, given the supply-demand mismatch in
the educational sphere in the country—there is simply just
so much talent in all corners of the country that was not

able to rise hitherto because of certain restrictions on access to information and opportunities, and not enough premier institutions to cater to this vast pool of talent. Until now, because of lack of access to opportunities, this section's demand never came through and the premier institutions kept going at their own pace. Today, because of the networking of the economy, access to information and opportunities has risen enormously, making the premier institutes incapable of serving this surge in demand and leading to quality talent springing up from all over the country.

For instance, at HDFC Bank, other than Sashidhar Jagdishan, none of the executive directors are from an IIT or IIM or a foreign university. They are all University of Mumbai graduates. The top-executive profile of the largest bank in the country by market cap is emblematic of the change that is underway in the country at large—the rise of corporate leaders from non-elite educational institutes.

Small-Town India and Rise of the Octopus

Contrary to what is generally believed, the growth in the financialization of small-town India is even more dramatic than what has taken place in the country's megacities. Thanks to Aadhaar and Jan Dhan accounts, a massive portion of the population came into the formal banking system for the first time since Independence. This has opened up multiple opportunities for them in the world of organized financial services. As you can see in the exhibit below, every geography type has witnessed rapid growth in credit off-take (at around 11 per cent per annum), especially in the last seven years. However, as per RBI data, credit growth data for banks in urban and semi-urban areas has far outpaced big-city credit growth (represented in the chart below as 'Metropolitan').

Exhibit 5.4: Credit Growth Takes Off in Regions Beyond Metros

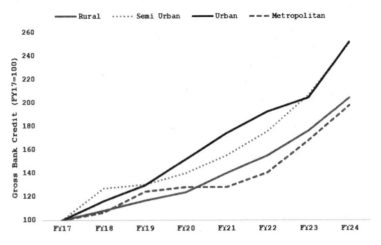

Source: Basic Statistical Return (BSR) 2, RBI's database on Indian Economy; here credit growth means growth in gross bank credit outstanding in Rs crore of Scheduled Commercial Banks; data normalized to 2017=100 for assessing growth

In fact, as we travel around India, raising assets for our portfolio management services franchise, we can see that in small-town India, owners of SME businesses have figured out for themselves that their land, their property and their gold will not be enough to fund them through retirement. The RBI's remarkably well-researched August 2017 Household Financial Committee report says that 95 per cent of Indian households' stock of wealth is in physical assets. As most investors in India now know, physical assets struggle to keep up even with the rate of inflation (and therefore cannot create wealth in real terms). Unfortunately for these SME owners, very few Indian couples have the wherewithal to retire with a corpus of Rs 15 crore ($2 mn) in financial assets and thus adequately fund a twenty-five-year upper middle-class retirement (assuming the need for a post-retirement annual income of Rs 50 lakh ($60K)).

The practical implication of this is that the smaller the town, the quicker the SME owner warms up to our offerings. So, using Tamil Nadu as an example, a pitch which takes an hour in Chennai takes 45 minutes in Coimbatore (population: 1.6 million), 40 minutes in Tiruppur (population: 0.8 million) and around 30 minutes in Erode (population: 0.5 million). We believe there are several reasons for this pattern (which we have seen in Maharashtra too):

- Financialization of savings has happened to a certain extent in big cities like Mumbai, Delhi, Bengaluru and Chennai. In the smaller cities, most SME owners have only a smattering of financial assets (usually fixed deposits and life insurance policies).

- The market for residential property and land still has some liquidity in the big cities—at least a few flats are being bought and sold in cities like Mumbai and Chennai. In the smaller cities, the market for real estate has frozen solid. There have been no deals all year long in several of the smaller cities we have visited.

- The audience that meets us in the bigger cities tends to have a greater proportion of people from the white-collar professions. They have a steady income and hence a greater sense of security. In the smaller cities, the audience consists mostly of SME owners who have to live by their wits. They are textile traders, spice traders, car dealers and local real estate developers. These people have to live with volatility in their enterprises and hence crave the security that comes from investing in a relatively predictable financial asset. We like to call such entrepreneurial business owners Octopuses. This is so due to the process of wealth accumulation that they are employing, whose effect is visible at two levels in the country—rural and urban.

The Small-Town Wealth Creation Model

Let's consider grain traders in a small town. For years these traders were doing business conventionally, and a large part of it informally. But with demonetization and GST, most of them have formalized their businesses and now have access to the formal banking channels. A smart grain trader now takes loans from banks to open a cold storage to increase the shelf life of his products and sell them at a later date when prices are higher. As a result, he generates a surplus over time from selling grain. He now uses this surplus to secure a two-wheeler dealership. As that dealership flourishes, he uses his enhanced surplus to open a car dealership.

By this time, the small trader has generated considerable clout within his town (financially as well as in terms of his social status). Leveraging this clout, he gets his son into the local municipal corporation (or zilla parishad). Over the next few years, his son rises in the local political hierarchy. Father and son then work together to get contracts for local road construction/ repair. Profits from these local construction contracts further enhance the family's surplus, which they can then use to become local real estate developers. Thus, over the course of a decade, a mini conglomerate is created, which consolidates its financial, social and political power in that town. This conglomerate will now steadily push its tentacles into every economically lucrative activity in that area—hence the term 'Octopus'.

Our travels across India over the past decade have shown us that:

- A town with less than 0.5 million people will have twenty such families, who will account for 80 per cent of the wealth in that town.
- A city with 1 million people will have fifty such families who will account for 80 per cent of the wealth in that city.

- A tier-2 city like Pune or Lucknow will have 100 to 300 such families who will account for 80 per cent of the wealth in that city; and
- Major metros like Mumbai and Delhi will have a few thousand such families who will account for 80 per cent of the wealth in that city.

Thus, at the national level, around 2,00,000 such families (or between 7,00,000 and 1 million individuals) end up controlling 80 per cent of India's wealth.

Urban Wealth-Creation Model

Whilst Octopuses in small-town India are owners of small businesses that go on to become mini-conglomerates, the big city Octopuses operate in a different way from their small-town cousins. In particular, they are likely to have a high skill quotient in terms of technical qualifications, which they will deploy to get well-paid jobs in India Inc. As India's leading companies continue gunning out profit growth of 15 per cent per annum, the number of highly paid executives who manage these companies continues to burgeon. To hold on to their best talent, these companies will:

(a) Pay Their Executives Well. The *Economic Times* says that in the listed company universe, there are 1,161 individuals in the country who have an annual pay packet of Rs 1 crore or more.[4]

(b) Give Their Executives Equity-Based Compensation, which will then compound with the share price of the company, thus implying, at the market-wide level, around four times growth in wealth every decade.

Furthermore, the most ambitious of the corporate Octopuses are likely to quit to create their own start-ups, where a combination of their equity ownership alongside venture capital or private equity funding could make them dollar millionaires in the span of a few years.

Thus, the big city octopuses will be a combination of listed-company owners (there are around 6000 such families in India), venture capital- and private equity-backed company owners (which we estimate number approximately 680[5]) and the senior talent working in these companies.

Examples of Super-Rich Families

Ghari: Ghari detergent from RSPL (previously Rohit Surfactants) is India's largest selling detergent brand. From its humble beginnings in Kanpur in Uttar Pradesh, RSPL's Ghari detergent today commands a share of approximately 20 per cent in the $3.75 billion detergent industry in India.[6] RSPL also has forayed into dairy, footwear, renewable energy (they have five wind power plants with an installed capacity of 50.1 MW) and real estate.[7] Had this Kanpur-based company been a listed entity, its owners would comfortably be dollar billionaires.

Dainik Bhaskar (DB Corp): The Bhopal-based Agarwal family started with just one Hindi daily back in 1958, called *Dainik Bhaskar*. Today, it is the most popular and circulated daily[8] in the entire country. Over the years, DB Corporation, controlled to this day by the Agarwal family, has sought to enter other verticals like power and real estate. Although they haven't been as successful in these ventures as in their print business, it is the entrepreneurial talent of this family that has made *Dainik Bhaskar* become what it is today. Within the media vertical, DB Corp has forayed into radio and digital media.[9] DB Corp's market cap is in the region of Rs 6,000 crore ($800 million), and the Agarwal family owns around 72 per cent[10] of the listed entity.

Rise of Talent From Oppressed Castes

> When the people of Sankarapadu entered Hindu society with no caste of their own and the most impure occupation of all, that of landless labourers, there was no question where their place would be: at the bottom, as despised outcastes. Outcastes are also called untouchables because they are supposed to be so ritually unclean that the slightest contact with them will defile even low-caste Hindus. Untouchables cannot share meals with others, much less intermarry with them, and are made to live apart from the rest of the village in a segregated colony on its outskirts. Sankarapadu became the untouchable colony of Polukonda, albeit an unusually remote one.
>
> —Sujatha Gidla in *Ants Among Elephants: An Untouchable Family and the Making of Modern India* (2017)

Historically, the oppressed castes in India have been given a raw deal—socially, financially, and at the workplace. Political ostracization has existed across the country and at varying levels of intensity. Caste-based discrimination has robbed a large swathe of Indian people of economic opportunities and reduced their opportunities to break free from poverty.

While affirmative action, which the Indian state has implemented since 1947 in favour of the hitherto discriminated castes, has helped, it is the democratization of opportunities over the past decade that has supercharged the economic emergence of non-upper castes.

For example, the data on workforce participation (which is defined as the number of people employed out of the total labour force, including the employed and unemployed) shows that the most disadvantaged castes have closed the gap with the rest of the population. In fact, the workforce participation for scheduled tribes in India is actually higher than that workforce participation for the rest of the country, at 559 per 1000 people versus 492 per 1000 people, respectively, in 2022 (see exhibit below).

Exhibit 5.5: The Most Disadvantaged Sections of Society are Progressing the Quickest in the Labour Market

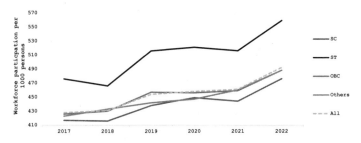

Source: Centre for Economic and Data Analysis (CEDA); continuous series in this data starts only after 2017; workforce participation here is calculated as the number of employed per 1000 people; this data is for caste-based workforce participation, keeping everything else constant (i.e., religion, gender, etc.)

This suggests that given an increasingly level playing field, some of the most historically disadvantaged segments of Indian society are rising faster than their more privileged counterparts. A somewhat similar phenomenon was also witnessed in the US, with Jews racing far ahead of their fellow American counterparts, especially in the economic boom that transformed America into a superpower in the quarter century after the end of World War II.

As new groups of entrepreneurs and professionals rise in India, it is highly likely that they will ramp up the intensity of competition for incumbent businesses run by the entrenched elites. We will discuss this emerging tussle amongst the 'Rulers' and the 'Challengers' further in the final chapter of the book.

Summary

The networking of India, digitally and physically, has democratized access to economic opportunities. This has helped new groups of people rise in the Indian economy. These newly ascendant people are neither based in India's megacities, nor are they graduates from elite universities, nor do they belong to the socially privileged castes. From India's smaller cities, from hundreds of local universities and from the less privileged castes, a new entrepreneurial and professional class is rising to grab the reins of power and privilege in India.

6

The Explosive Ascent of Peninsular India

Consider a child born in India. Firstly, this child is far less likely to be born in southern India than in northern India, given the former's lower rates of population growth.

But let's assume she is. In which case, she is far less likely to die in the first year of her life given the lower infant mortality rates in south India compared with the rest of the country.

She is more likely to get vaccinated, less likely to lose her mother during childbirth, more likely to have access to child services and receive better early childhood nutrition.

She is also more likely to celebrate her fifth birthday, find a hospital or a doctor in case she falls sick and eventually live a slightly longer life.

She will go to school and stay in school longer—she will more likely go to college as well. She is less likely to be involved in agriculture for economic sustenance . . .

She will also go on to be a mother to fewer children, who in turn will be healthier and more educated than her.

—R.S. Nilakantan, author of *South vs North: India's Great Divide*, quoted by the BBC in September 2022.

The Rise of Peninsular India

One of the privileges of our profession is the extensive travel we do in the course of our work across all parts of India. Not only that, but our line of work also puts us in contact with interesting people from all walks of life—from billionaires who own large companies to dealers who run small shops to their employees who deal on a daily basis with the ordinary Indian citizen. We look forward to these discussions, both as a means by which to learn about the companies in which we invest and as a barometer of how the country is changing. Often, therefore, our first discussion when we land in a new city is with the taxi driver who takes us from the airport to our first meeting.

For over a decade now, we have been seeing that our discussions with taxi drivers in south India last longer and have become more meaningful than our discussions with taxi drivers elsewhere in the country. Often, these discussions veer towards the subjects the taxi driver's kids are studying at university or the jobs they have taken up in the software industry or in the pharmaceutical or manufacturing sector. Often we find ourselves discussing with south Indian taxi drivers subjects as diverse as house prices, interest rates and the rising influence of social media, IPL teams' spending on star cricketers, the latest movies and—this is a pan-Indian favourite—the growing assertiveness of their wives and daughters. In the south Indian taxi driver's vehicle, we will usually spot both that day's English newspaper and a regional newspaper. These taxi drivers—earning as they usually do between Rs 3–6 lakhs ($4000–8000) per annum—typify the rising affluence and aspirations of Indian citizens, but the additional breadth of their knowledge and thought speaks of the greater rise of south India as compared with the rest of the country.

Per capita income in the seven 'southern' states (Tamil Nadu, Telangana, Andhra, Kerala, Karnataka, Goa, and Maharashtra) has grown at an average 10 per cent CAGR between FY14 and FY23. These states, which account for 30 per cent of India's population and 45 per cent of India's GDP, now have an average per capita income of approximately Rs 3.07 lakh ($3700), more than 50 per cent higher than the rest of India's. A decade ago, the corresponding 'South vs Rest' gap was 35 per cent (see exhibit below). To be more specific, in terms of per capita income, Telangana tops the list, at over Rs 3.5 lakh (more than $4K) per annum.[1]

Exhibit 6.1: Average Per Capita Income of the Southern States is Zooming Past The Rest of India's

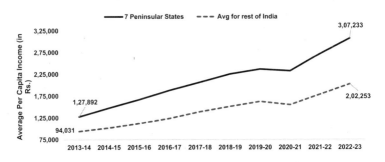

Source: Ministry of Statistical and Programme Implementation (MOSPI), Parliamentary Query document; the 7 peninsular states here are Telangana, Andhra, Maharashtra, Goa, Tamil Nadu, Kerala, and Karnataka; Rest of India consists of all the other states and union territories; to the due unavailability of data for many states for 2023–24, data has been considered only until 2022–23; financial years are considered

What is even more intriguing about this scenario is that while infrastructure development can be seen all across the country (see Chapter 3), not all regions are benefiting equally from it. The south, which has always been at the vanguard of India's social and economic progress, is increasingly racing far ahead of the rest of the country. There are three dimensions along which the south is becoming a more powerful economy than the rest of India:

Per Capita Income in the seven southern states has grown at an incredible average 10 per cent CAGR over FY14–23 to now reach approximately Rs 3.07 lakh ($3700). The corresponding figure for the rest of India is 8 per cent. A 2 percentage-point differential in income growth means that from being 35 per cent richer than the rest of the country in FY14, the seven southern states are now 50 per cent richer.

More Equal Dispersion of Wealth among the southern states. As they move towards becoming second-world economies (in terms of per capita income), the disparity of wealth between these seven states is narrowing too—i.e., the southern states are becoming more uniformly prosperous. This can be seen in the exhibit below, which uses the coefficient of variation (i.e., standard deviation/average) as a measure of dispersion. In contrast, the states in the rest of India are becoming more dissimilar as the country continues to grow at a healthy rate overall.

Exhibit 6.2: Disparity in Per Capita Income Among Constituent States is Remarkably More Elevated in the North Than in the South

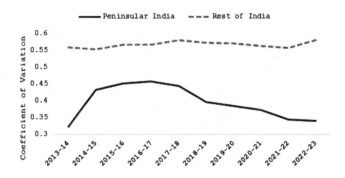

Source: Ministry of Statistical and Programme Implementation (MOSPI); coefficient of variation calculated as standard deviation of per capita incomes of all the peninsular states (as identified in previous exhibit) divided by the average per capita income of the southern states for each year, and similarly for the rest of India; the higher the coefficient of variation, the higher the disparity in the per capita incomes of the states considered; due to unavailability of enough data points for the year 2023–24, data only until 2022–23 has been considered; financial years are considered

- Large Clusters Capable of Sustained Economic Development preferred by both Indian and foreign companies. Such companies naturally prefer to set up operations in parts of the country where skilled labour is readily available, where the transport infrastructure is well established and where the rule of law can be taken for granted. The south already has several economic clusters where per capita income is above Rs 2.5 lakhs ($3000) per annum—Goa, Karnataka (specifically, the area around Bengaluru), Tamil Nadu (specifically, the areas around Chennai, Hosur and Coimbatore), Telangana (specifically, the area around Hyderabad). The north, in contrast, just has Delhi (more generally, the National Capital Region spanning Gurgaon and Manesar in Haryana and Noida in Uttar Pradesh) and Gujarat, where per capita income is above Rs 2.5 lakh ($3000). With the south already having more economic clusters, both Indian and foreign companies prefer to set up their new Indian operations in the south. In the north, barring the National Capital Region and Gujarat, one rarely hears about new operations being set up. The result of this can be seen in exhibit below—a booming southern state like Telangana has more than doubled its per capita income in the past six years.

Exhibit 6.3: Growth in Per Capita Income in Telangana Far Outstrips That of UP

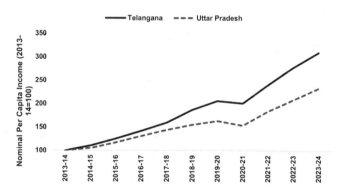

Source: Marcellus Investment Managers using data from Ministry of Statistical and Programme Implementation (MOSPI); per capita incomes for both the states rebased to 100 at the beginning of the period for better comparability of their growth rates; financial years are considered

Tamil Nadu as a Microcosm of the Stellar Rise of South India

The celebrated journalist and award-winning author Harish Damodaran has captured the factors underpinning south India's economic ascendancy better than almost anyone else in the mainstream media. Using the case study of Tamil Nadu, Damodaran explains:

Tamil Nadu . . . is India's No.1 state in terms of economic complexity, measured by the diversity of its gross domestic product (GDP) and employment profile.

The table below shows the farm sector's share in TN's gross value added (GVA; i.e. GDP net of product taxes and subsidies) and also in its employed labour force to be well below the national average. The lower dependence on agriculture is matched by the higher shares of industry, services and construction in its economy relative to all-India.

Table 6.1: Tamil Nadu's Sector-Wise Shares in GVA and the Workforce are more Decentralized than All-India Figures in 2022–23

Particulars	Gross Value Added *		Workforce	
	All India	Tamil Nadu	All India	Tamil Nadu
Agriculture	18.19%	12.55%	45.76%	28.87%
Industry**	18.80%	22.69%	12.27%	17.88%
Construction	8.84%	11.70%	13.03%	18.04%
Services	54.18%	53.05%	28.94%	35.21%

Source: National Accounts Statistics, Periodic Labour Force Survey (sourced from the Indian Express); at basic prices, where GVA is net of product taxes and subsidies; includes manufacturing, mining, electricity and utilities

. . . Another indicator of economic complexity is agriculture itself. About 45.3 per cent of TN's farm GVA comes from the livestock subsector, the highest for any state and way above the 30.2 per cent all-India average. Not surprisingly, TN is home to India's largest private dairy company (Hatsun Agro Product), broiler enterprise (Suguna Foods), egg processor (SKM Group) and also 'egg capital' (Namakkal).

TN has just a handful of large business houses with annual revenues in excess of Rs 15,000 crore: TVS, Murugappa, MRF, Amalgamations and Apollo Hospitals. Even they are not in the league of Tata, Reliance, Aditya Birla, Adani, Mahindra, JSW, Vedanta, Bharti, Infosys, HCL or Wipro, as far as turnover goes.

TN's economic transformation has been brought about not by so-called Big Capital as much as medium-scale businesses with turnover ranging from Rs 100 crore to

Rs 5000 crore (some, like Hatsun and Suguna, have graduated to the next Rs 5000–10,000 crore level). Its industrialisation has also been more spread out and decentralised, via the development of clusters.[2]

Why has the south surged ahead of the rest of India?

The market alone cannot determine the appropriate level and location of public infrastructure investment, or rules for the settlement of labor disputes, or the degree of airline and trucking regulation, or occupational health and safety standards. Each one of these questions is 'value-laden' to some extent, and must be referred to the political system. And if that system is going to adjudicate these conflicting interests fairly and in a way that receives the consent of all of the major actors within the economy, it must be democratic. A dictatorship could resolve such conflicts in the name of economic efficiency, but the smooth functioning of a modern economy depends on the willingness of its many interdependent social components to work together. **If they do not believe in the legitimacy of the adjudicator, if there is no trust in the system, there will be no active and enthusiastic cooperation of the sort required to make the system as a whole function smoothly** . . . Shared cultural values build trust and lubricate, so to speak, the interaction of citizens with one another.

—Francis Fukuyama in *The End of History and the Last Man* (1992)

In his landmark publication *The End of History and the Last Man*, Francis Fukuyama has explained how trust in a society is intricately linked to the development of large industrial organizations. If people trust each other to follow an unwritten set of social rules (which are implicitly understood by all), then doing business costs less. On the other hand, people who do not trust each other will end up cooperating only under the aegis of a formal set of rules and regulations, which will impose on the ongoing costs of doing business.

Based on our travels across India over the past fifteen years, south India comes across as a higher-trust society than the rest of the country. Part of the reason for this seems to be that major conflicts around caste seem to have already played out in south India by the 1960s. As V.S. Naipaul explains in *India: A Million Mutinies Now*, (1990):

> Twenty years after the independence of India . . . After my introduction to the brahmin culture of the South, this was my introduction to the revolt of the South: the revolt of South against North, non-brahmin against brahmin, the racial revolt of dark against fair, Dravidian against Aryan. The revolt had begun long before; the brahmin world I had come upon in 1962 was one that had already been undermined.
>
> The party that had won the state election in 1967 was the DMK, the Dravidian Progressive Movement. It had deep roots; it had its own prophet and its own politician-leader, men who were its equivalents of Gandhi and Nehru, men whose careers had run strangely parallel with the careers of the mainstream Indian independence leaders . . . And what that victory in 1967 meant was that the culture to which I had been introduced . . . the culture which had appeared whole and mysterious and ancient to me, had been overthrown.

While the caste system still likely prevails in south India, it isn't an all-encompassing feature of daily business life. In contrast, both in our lived experience and according to sociologists, barring the National Capital Region, caste and upper-caste dominance still seem to be central to daily business life in north India. As Harish Damodaran explains in *India's New Capitalists* (2008):

> Non-Brahmin mobilizations in the Madras and Bombay Presidency areas from the turn of the last century, in fact,

had a dual impact. Firstly, they created a middle class with a reasonably broad social base. Secondly, by redefining and tweaking conventional social hierarchies, they forced the Brahmins and other upper castes to explore alternative career paths and become entrepreneurs themselves in the bargain.

Besides education and affirmative action, the factor that has contributed to a considerable 'democratization of capital' in the South is the absence of stranglehold over business by traditional mercantile and banking communities. Not that they did not exist; but the Chettiars and Komatis were nowhere as overbearing in the money and commodity markets as the ubiquitous northern Bania.

One specific manifestation of south India being a higher-trust society than the rest of the country is that on average, across the seven southern states, the rate of murder per lakh of population is 1.9, whereas the average for India as a whole is 2.8.[3]

Another consequence of the south being a less fractured society with higher levels of trust is the nature of capitalism in the region, which is more inclusive than that in the rest of India. Harish Damodaran lays out this contrast eloquently in his book *India's New Capitalists*, in the context of the sugarcane industry:

> . . . this 'inclusive capitalism' has been more a feature of southern and, to some extent, western India. Take, for instance, the sugar industry in the South, which cannot possibly be identified with any particular community. Thus, we have EID Parry (Nattukottai Chettiar), Sakthi Sugars, Bannari Amman Sugars and Dharani Sugars (Gounders), Thiru Arooran Sugars (Mudaliar), Ponni Sugars (Brahmin), Rajshree Sugars (Naidu), Andhra Sugars and KCP Sugar (Kammas), GMR Industries (Komati), Gayatri Sugars (Reddy), Kothari Sugars (Gujarati Bania/Jain) and Empee Sugars (Ezhava).

This is not so in the North, where businessmen tend to be uniformly Bania-Marwaris or Khatris. The Jats (both Hindu and Sikh), Yadavs, Gujjars, and other intermediate castes produce the bulk of its sugarcane, paddy, wheat, cotton, oilseeds and milk, but rarely does one find sugar millers, branded rice makers, grain exporters, textile tycoons, solvent extractors and dairy processors from these communities.

Things are better in the West, where the co-operative movement has enabled peasant castes like the Marathas and Patidars to make a successful entry into industry.

The networking of India and the advent of GST has, if anything, hastened the pace at which the south is pulling away from and ahead of the rest of the country, because:

- Pre-GST firms had some tax incentives to locate in tax-exempt northern states like Himachal Pradesh and Uttarakhand. Now these tax incentives are no longer relevant.
- When India's road and telephone infrastructure was rickety, firms got incentives to locate their factories closer to their customers. The pre-GST indirect tax system also encouraged this. In the post-GST world, with high-quality highways rippling across the land, firms now locate factories where they have access to skilled labour and where law-and-order issues are not present. That swings the balance in favour of south India.

Effectively, the south is now India's domestic equivalent of an efficient east Asian economy, and the rest of India is increasingly going to 'import' what it needs from the south. Ironically, the south's enhanced economic potency seems likely to interplay with a historic political decision taken in 1971 to create a thorny problem in the years to come.

The Looming Spectre of 'Delimitation'

Delimitation means the process of fixing the number of seats and boundaries of territorial constituencies in each State for the Lok Sabha. The Constitution says that the number of seats in the Lok Sabha as well as its division into territorial constituencies shall be readjusted after each Census. This 'delimitation process' is performed by the 'Delimitation Commission' that is set up under an act of Parliament. Such exercises were carried out after the 1951, 1961 and 1971 Census.

As explained by The Hindu newspaper: The number of seats in the Lok Sabha based on the 1951, 1961 and 1971 Census was fixed at 494, 522 and 543, when the population was 36, 44 and 55 crores respectively. This broadly translates to an average population of 7.3, 8.4 and 10.1 lakh per seat respectively.'[4]

However, the number of Lok Sabha seats has been frozen as per the 1971 Census. This was done through the Forty-second Amendment Act until the year 2000 and was extended by the Eighty-fourth Amendment Act until 2026. Hence, the population based on which the number of seats is allocated refers to the population as per the 1971 Census. This number will be re-adjusted based on the first Census after 2026.

In the normal course of events, the delimitation process for the number of seats and boundaries of territorial constituencies would have happened based on the Census of 2031 as it would have been the first Census after 2026. However, with the 2021 Census now being postponed and the year 2026 nearing, there have been discussions about the impending delimitation exercise.

Currently, the peninsular states account for a third of the seats in the Lok Sabha (179 of the total 543 seats[5]) although these states, as has been discussed earlier, account for half of India's GDP and thus contribute half of the Indian Exchequer's revenues. If after the delimitation exercise is carried out, the peninsular states' seat share in the Lok Sabha drops to, say, a quarter, it is likely to trigger protest. Peninsular Indians could ask 'Why should we contribute half of India's tax revenues if we account for only a quarter of the seats in the Lok Sabha?'. The rest of the country seems likely to counter that 'democracy means one vote per person irrespective of where that person resides in India'. With no easy answers to this thorny debate, the south's economic ascendancy could end up creating a Hobson's choice.

Summary

Peninsular India's per capita income has grown at an average 10 per cent CAGR between FY14 and FY23. These states, which account for 30 per cent of India's population and 45 per cent of India's GDP, now have an average per capita income of around Rs 3.07 lakh ($3700), 50 per cent higher than that of the rest of India's. As peninsular India pulls away economically from the rest of the country, we see rising fortunes of booming states like Maharashtra, Karnataka, Telangana and Tamil Nadu creating a Hobson's choice for India as the nation nears the delimitation exercise in 2026.

7

China's Unravelling Creates a $300-billion+ Opportunity

China absolutely faces deindustrialization and deurbanization on a scale that is nothing less than mythic. It almost certainly faces political disintegration and even de-civilization. And it does so against a backdrop of an already disintegrating demography.

—Peter Zeihan in *The End of the World Is Just the Beginning: Mapping the Collapse of Globalization* (2022)

Exhibit 7.1: India and China's Quarterly Real GDP Growth (YoY) for the Last 19 Years

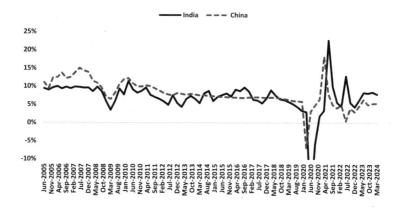

Source: Bloomberg; India's real GDP growth pegged at 2004–05 prices before 2011, and then at 2011–12 prices; China's real GDP growth rate pegged at 2005–09 prices until 2009, 2010–14 prices until 2014, and 2015 prices thereafter to date

Introduction: China's and India's Contrasting Fortunes

What happened in the 1990s removed many of the restrictions on both foreign and domestic companies. Before, domestic Chinese who wanted to set up anything larger than a cottage industry had to go through elaborate and at times bizarre steps to function legally. Banks could not lend to private, non-state owned entities, and private organizations could legally employ a handful of people . . .

In 1992, the United States was about to plunge into the Internet revolution, and the European Union was celebrating its giddy first days. But in China, the economy – for all the ferment of the past decade—was still barely in the twentieth century . . .

When Deng reignited the economic development in 1992, no one could have possibly envisioned that within 15 years, society would be radically altered. It was as if Deng had sprinkled growth pixie dust everywhere he went and the results were skyscrapers, roads, factories, ships, airports, and the entire phantasmagoric spectrum of the modern world.

—Zachary Karabell in *Superfusion: How China and America Became One Economy and Why the World's Prosperity Depends on It* (2009)

The rise of China is arguably the key development that shaped the American economic discourse of the late twentieth and early twenty-first centuries. The underpinnings of the rise of an economic behemoth with immense fire power have been rooted in the economic reforms that China witnessed under Deng Xiaoping.

Prior to 1976, the year when Mao Zedong passed away, the Chinese economy was shackled by the short-sighted and widely prevalent ideals of communism that regarded the free-market economy with derision and scoffed at even the slightest mention of capitalism. In 1978, Deng Xiaoping came to power in China. He realized that for China to grow and gain economic prosperity, something had to change, and it had to change quickly. China at the beginning of the decade of the 1980s was largely an agrarian economy, and therefore the first set of reforms that was implemented pertained to agriculture. These agri reforms effectively revolutionized the occupation that the majority of the Chinese citizens were employed in. This agenda of reforms faced a major hiccup in 1989 with the protests at Tiananmen Square. However, in front of a global television audience, these protests were quashed brutally and swiftly by the incumbent government. While to the world this spectacle may have looked like a major hurdle for China to overcome to continue on its path to economic reforms, within China it was forgotten and overcome pretty quickly, given the level of brutality the Chinese people had become accustomed to in the decades prior, when Mao Zedong ruled the country.

In fact, post-Tiananmen, China's economic reforms went into a hyper-drive from 1992 onwards, when Deng undertook a celebrated tour of southern China visiting cities' such as Shenzhen, Zhuhai, Guangzhou and Shanghai and saying that 'those who do not promote reform should be brought down from their leadership positions'. This emphasis on reform continued even after his passing away in 1997. Deng's immediate successors, Jiang Remin and Zhu Rongji, furthered Deng's idea of economic reforms and the clear decoupling of the country's political and economic agendas. In stark contrast to how the Western countries witnessed their own economic renaissance, which often went hand in hand with political upheaval, China was successfully able to decouple economic progress from political progress. In fact, the Chinese state promised its people economic and financial stability at the cost of their freedom to speak against the power centre in Beijing. For the world's most populous nation, this deal worked just fine, given that for nearly four decades after World War II the people's lives had been characterized by neither economic nor political freedom. As the reforms progressed through the 1990s and the first decade of the twenty-first century, more than 200 million Chinese people shifted to newly created city centres in pursuit of higher wages and a better life.

Not only did the economic reforms expedited under Deng Xiaoping, Jiang Remin and Zhu Rongji give confidence to Chinese companies, the Western world too started believing in China's ability to produce sustained prosperity. The most notable early manifestation of this confidence was the establishment of a Kentucky Fried Chicken (KFC) outlet in China in 1987. KFC was where Chinese factory workers began to satiate their hunger for both food and Western capitalism, and it was emblematic of the free-market economy and the financial fruits thereof for everyone.

A slew of reforms followed, making access to financing for up-and-coming industries easy via bank loans, reduction in bureaucratic paperwork and general allowance for private enterprises to scale up and employ tens of thousands of people. All these changes, in retrospect, seem the only logical way forward for an economy to grow, and there seems nothing extraordinary about them. But what was extraordinary was that nearly all of these changes took place in a fifteen-year period, between the mid-1980s and the end of the twentieth century.

The natural culmination of these changes was an economy growing at a minimum rate of 10 per cent per annum and hungry for more growth. A natural climax of these reforms was China eventually joining the World Trade Organization (WTO) in 2002–03. In fact, more than a decade prior, Deng himself had laid the groundwork for this by signing the General Agreement on Tariff and Trade (GATT), the precursor to the WTO.

To their credit, the Chinese leadership understood the need for swift economic transformation, especially in the wake of the rapid growth demonstrated by their east Asian neighbours through the 1980s and 1990s. And yet the Chinese leadership, having witnessed the fall of the Soviet Union and the unravelling thereafter of the Russian economy, wanted to open China to the broader world gradually. As a result, China did not allow the IMF and the World Bank to pressure it to prematurely open up its economy to the pulls and pressures of global free trade.[1]

Naturally, after China's joining the WTO, as the world and the US shifted its focus to China, companies prospered across the globe as they shifted the majority of their manufacturing to this country. Word spread around the world that the Chinese could make the same products at scale and at a fraction of the cost in the West.

China's incredible prowess in globally competitive low-cost manufacturing is reflected in its economic statistics. In 1978, China's output accounted for roughly 0.5 per cent of the global economic output. Thirty years later, this figure had jumped to 10 per cent.[2]

An unintended yet profound consequence of this was the loss of blue-collar jobs not just in the US but across most of the Western world. As companies found an opportunity to reduce labour costs by shifting production and operations to China, a majority of the factory jobs in the US, specifically, shifted en masse to China, much to the dismay of middle-class factory workers in America. This led to resentment among the Americans, who believed they were being given a raw deal even as multinational Western corporations began generating outsized profits from making in China and selling in the West.

The anger and distrust of Americans who believed that they had got a raw deal from the rise of China in the global economy reached its zenith in 2016, when Donald Trump, the Republican candidate for the post of President, locked into this mass discontent and was elected with a thumping majority. What followed thereafter was a slew of tariffs on products coming from China, sparking the beginning of a trade war emanating from a mix of distrust of Chinese intentions on the part of Americans and America's perceived need to arrest China's meteoric economic growth.

By 2024, the annual poll conducted by Pew Research Center on how Americans view China started throwing up results that pointed to the deep distrust between the two nations:

> Around four-in-ten Americans (42 per cent) say China is an enemy of the U.S. This is fewer than the 50 per cent who describe China as a competitor but a slight increase from the 38 per cent of Americans who described China as an enemy last year. It is also the largest share who have described China as an enemy since we began asking the question.[3]

Part of the reason why American hostility towards China has amped up in recent years is the Covid pandemic of 2020–2021. By and large, the Western view remains that Covid arose in the Wuhan province of China in 2019 and that fewer lives would have been lost had China forewarned the rest of the world sooner about Covid. Post-Covid, Sino-American relations dropped to a new low after China's alleged spying activities (such as the Chinese spy balloon, which flew across America in March 2023, apparently collecting intelligence from several sensitive US military sites)[4] made the US administration even more wary of the Middle Kingdom.

To add further fuel to the flames in the Sino-American relationship, the elections to the Chinese Communist Party's politburo in 2022 resulted in the exit of all economic reformers from the politburo. The reformers were replaced by military men and spies loyal to Xi Jinping.[5]

Western efforts to contain China have centred on the use of tariff barriers and the banning of the export of technologically advanced equipment from the West to China, for example, the extreme ultra-violet lithography machines used to manufacture the cutting-edge semiconductors used in the latest iPhones. In addition to the economic pain created by these tariffs and sanctions, China is undergoing a long overdue real estate bust (in the wake of Xi Jinping saying that he doesn't want to see house prices rising further), which in turn is playing havoc with the balance sheets of China's largest lenders.

Even as China experiences social, political and economic turmoil, the Indian economy seems to be in fine fettle—the opening exhibit in this chapter is a visual illustration of the contrasting fortunes of the world's two most populous nations. The government of India's tax collections are growing at 18 per cent year on year,[6] more than twice as fast as the country's nominal GDP growth. Credit growth in the banking system is running at 20 per cent YoY,[7] the highest in a decade. Utility vehicle sales, two-wheeler and three-wheeler sales are growing at 26 per cent, 13.3 per cent and 42 per cent YoY, respectively.[8]

More importantly for India, as China unravels the possibility grows with every passing month that large chunks of the

Chinese economy will migrate to other countries, including (but not restricted to) India. As Peter Zeihan writes in his recent bestselling book *The End of the World is Just The Beginning: Mapping the Collapse of Globalization* (2022):

> China absolutely faces deindustrialization and deurbanization on a scale that is nothing less than mythic . . . India, with all its endless internal variation, hopes to take a bite out of everything.

The question, therefore, is which segments of the Chinese economy India can aspire to yank away. Our research points to three large sectors where India potentially has a relative advantage vis-a-vis the other highly competitive Asian economies:

- Smartphones and the ancillaries related to it,
- Active pharmaceutical ingredients (APIs) and the ancillaries related to it, and
- Medical devices and the ancillaries related to it.

Smartphones and Associated Ancillaries

The global market size of the smartphone industry is around $608bn.[9] China's smartphone exports account for roughly half of the global smartphone industry,[10] i.e., they amount to around $300bn. In contrast, India exports smartphones[11] worth $16 bn. India's own domestic smartphone market is around $44 bn,[12] of which approximately $1.6 bn's worth is imported from China.[13]

What are India's Relative Competitive Advantages in this Sector?

In other words, why do we believe India can be competitive in the large-scale manufacture of smartphones? Though the gap between India and China's exports in smartphones is massive, India's imports of smartphones from China have been consistently falling for several reasons, a major one being the $1.1 bn-per-annum of production-linked incentives (PLI)[14] that has helped shift the manufacture of India's domestically consumed smartphones from China to India itself. Under the PLI scheme, the Government has encouraged domestic companies and establishments to set up manufacturing units with the government providing financial incentives to these units on incremental sales. In mobile phones specifically, India has already begun challenging China's hegemony.

Over and above the domestic consumption of smartphones, we already know from Apple's announcements that: (a) in FY24, it has exported around $14 bn's worth of iPhones from India[15] and plans to shift a significant part of its iPhone production to India over the next couple of years; (b) it plans to make its AirPods in India; and (c) it has had trouble in making the remaining $100 bn[16] worth of iPhones in factories in China.

Opportunity Size: According to a Bloomberg report, Apple plans to shift 25 per cent of its iPhone production to India by 2025,[17] which amounts to over $25 bn (i.e., 25 per cent of the total iPhone production worth over $100 bn in China). This $25 bn-per-annum of iPhones (iPads and AirPods are over and above this) will give India an opportunity worth $40 bn per annum in the broader smartphone manufacturing sector over the next couple of years.

In the longer term, if we assume that a fourth of China's exports shifts to India over the next decade and the Indian domestic market continues to grow at 12 per cent per annum (at a nominal GDP growth rate), an opportunity of close to $170 bn will be created in India in the smartphone industry over the next ten years.

Have We Seen Investments Being Announced in this Space?

- Already, China's largest mobile phone maker, the BBK group, is starting production of its Oppo, Vivo and Realme smartphones[18] in partnership with a local Indian contract manufacturer (Dixon Technologies), despite Oppo and Vivo's existing capacities in India.
- Major smartphone giants like Apple and Samsung, along with their contract manufacturers, are set to receive approximately $530 mn in incentives[19] from the Government of India for meeting production linked targets.
- The electronics manufacturing industry is demanding more incentives under the PLI scheme (to the tune of approximately $4.2 bn[20]) to support the growing demand under this category overall, and specifically in the light industrial, knowledge-intensive sectors like smartphone manufacturing.

APIs and Associated Ancillaries

Active pharmaceutical ingredients (APIs) are the critical chemical molecules in a medicine that gives the medicine its potency. While medicines are a combination of APIs, colouring, flavouring and other excipients, the most valuable component of a medicine is its API.

The global market size[21] for APIs is around $240 bn. Chinese exports account for 40 per cent[22] of this market, or around $96 bn. India's domestic API market is around $18 bn,[23] of which a staggering $12 bn, approximately, is imported from China,[24] accounting for nearly 70 per cent of India's total domestic API market.

What are India's Relative Competitive Advantages in this Sector?

As the West gets increasingly apprehensive about its dependence on China for APIs, the next natural preferred location of choice for API production would be India, given: (a) the production capacity that already exists in the country; (b) the process chemistry knowhow that already exists in the country and (c) the fact that no other countries, barring India and China, produce APIs on a large scale.

A second dimension to consider is that not only can India displace China to some extent as an API supplier to the West, but India can also reduce its own dependence on China for APIs.

Opportunity Size: If we assume that over the next decade a fourth of Chinese APIs (having grown at an average 3 per cent, in-line with world nominal GDP growth rate for the next ten years) exports transfer to India, and India's domestic consumption increases steadily at 12 per cent per annum (at nominal GDP growth rate), the sector has the potential to expand to $80 bn of annual production in India a decade hence.

Have We Seen Investments Being Announced in this Space?

- The government of India approved a PLI scheme of around $2 bn in 2021.[25] To this end, thirty-five APIs, in which India's import dependence (mainly on China) is 90 per cent, are now being manufactured in thirty-two different plants in India. Around fifty Indian companies in this space have so far benefited from this scheme.
- As a result, in 2023, production facilities for twenty-two key bulk drug's[26] pivotal for life-saving medicines, have already been commissioned in the country.

- Laurus Labs, a company involved in production of APIs for generic drugs, has invested $600 mn[27] each in API manufacturing and formulation facilities until now.

Medical Devices and Associated Ancillaries

Medical devices, from syringes, cannulas and stents at the smaller end to the electro-cardiograms, X-ray machines and dialysis machines at the larger end, are as critical to modern medical treatment as medicines. The global market size for medical devices is around $550 bn (an average of the numbers presented in the following reports: Mordor Intelligence,[28] Expert Market Research,[29] Fortune Business Insights[30]). Of this, Chinese exports are around $110 bn.[31] India's domestic medical devices market[32] is around $15 bn, of which imports are $11.5 bn,[33] implying that domestic production amounts to less than $4 bn.

What are India's Relative Competitive Advantages in this Sector?

Given the disparity in size between India's and China's medical device industries, clearly India cannot be cost competitive in this sector even with PLIs[34] kicking in. However, India's trump card is the wariness on the part of Western governments to rely on China for diagnostic and therapeutic medical devices. In 2016, therapeutic devices (like orthopaedic appliances and parts, hearing aids, artificial joints, pacemakers, etc.), which are typically either inserted in the human body or are at least in close contact with it, accounted for around 31 per cent of all medical devices exported by China. In fact, both therapeutic and diagnostic equipment constitute about 52 per cent of all medical devices exported[35] by the country.

The increasingly erratic behaviour of China's legal system in dealing with entrepreneurs who are not in Xi Jinping's good books has also alarmed multinational medical device manufacturers and made them wake up to the fact that protection of the intellectual property embedded in advanced medical devices is likely to be non-existent in China. As a result, Western manufacturers and users of medical devices are keen to reduce their dependence on China and make cost a secondary consideration. This gives India an opportunity to grow its domestic production from the current pitifully small figure of $4 bn (in the context of a $500 bn-plus global industry).

Opportunity Size: Even if one assumes that over the next decade, only a fourth of China's exports migrates to India and India's domestic consumption of medical equipment continues to grow at 12 per cent per annum (i.e., nominal GDP growth), a decade hence this sector could be reaching $70 bn per annum in size.

Have We Seen Investments Being Announced in this Space?

- The government of India's website lists multinationals[36] such as Baxter, Abbott, 3M, Braun and Boston Scientific as 'major investors' in India.
- The PLI scheme for medical devices[37] lists multiple companies. It also lists the products that can be made under this scheme. These include larger devices like X-ray machines and dialysis machines as well as implant devices like periphery and carotid stents and cerebral spinal fluid shunts, among others.
- In July 2022, Godrej Appliances launched[38] its new InsuliCool product range—Godrej InsuliCool and Godrej InsuliCool+—which are innovative cooling solutions especially designed for insulin storage in order to address the challenge faced by diabetes patients in storing insulin at the recommended temperatures.
- In September 2021, Siemens Healthineers announced[39] that molecular testing kits would be manufactured at its Vadodara unit in Gujarat.

Why We Shouldn't Get Carried Away by 'China+1'

Notwithstanding the aforementioned opportunities, and in spite of growing Western aversion towards China, a manufacturing renaissance in the Indian context will take a lot of hard work both on the part of the manufacturers and on the part of the state and central governments. This is largely on account of three key issues when it comes to manufacturing in India:

- For a relatively low per-capita-income country (around US$ 2500 annually) India's wage rates for unskilled workers are relatively high. For instance, the minimum monthly wage in Maharashtra is $200,[40] more than four times the rate in Bangladesh ($50[41] per month). Unfortunately for India, several states have even higher minimum wages than those stipulated by Maharashtra. This naturally renders labour-intensive manufacturing largely uncompetitive in the country vis-à-vis its relatively cheaper neighbours.

- Indian manufacturers, especially manufacturers who are SMEs, also have to contend to with the higher cost of capital prevalent in India relative to the highly competitive east Asian and south-east Asian economies. At a time when the benchmark prime lending rate at India's largest bank, State Bank of India, is in the mid-teens,[42] the corresponding loan prime rate in China is sub-4 per cent.[43] One of the key drivers of India's high cost of capital is high government borrowings, which drive up the cost of capital in India. Effectively, sovereign borrowing crowds out private sector borrowing in India.[44]

- Thanks to India being a densely populated country criss-crossed by many rivers (which end up creating large, fertile flood plains highly conducive for agriculture), India also has to contend with paucity of land for industrial purposes.[45] As a result, access to industrial land for building new factories (i.e. greenfield projects) is tightly controlled by state governments. This in turn not only makes it hard to get large tracts of land for new factories, but it also drives up the price of land for brownfield projects.

With land, labour and capital being inordinately expensive in India (relative to other emerging Asian economies), India has struggled for many decades now to build a manufacturing sector that can compete in the global market. Instead, free-market forces have pushed India in the direction in which the country has a relative competitive advantage, namely, the use of its brains to create knowledge-intensive products (like pharmaceuticals) and services (like IT services). Year after year, India outpaces China in the export of services. For example, India's services exports grew by 11.4 per cent in 2023, far outpacing China's growth in this segment.[46]

To address India's decades-old weakness in manufacturing exports, the government of India has introduced a PLI scheme to the tune of Rs 2 trillion ($25 billion).[47] Under this scheme, eligible companies receive financial incentives based on their incremental sales from products manufactured in India. The PLI scheme offers various benefits, including concessions on import and export duties, tax rebates, affordable land and support for anchor investors managing new projects.

However, such is the scale of the handicap that Indian manufacturers face due to the high costs of land, labour and capital that the PLI scheme has succeeded in galvanizing only one sector—namely, mobile phones.[48] In other sectors, companies participating in the PLI scheme have faced additional administrative burdens in complying with the reporting and documentation requirements[49] and funding constraints. Hence, while we are excited by the opportunities created for India by the unravelling of the Sino-American relationship, we have had to keep in check our expectations as to how much we can capitalize on China's woes. The table below summarizes the opportunities in the three critical sectors discussed in this chapter.

Table 7.1: Market-Sizing the 'China Unravelling' Opportunity for India (Units are in $bn)

Industry	Indigenisation in India of goods exported by China (grown at 3.5% p.a. over 10 years)	Current domestic production 10 years hence (grown at 12% p.a.)	Total expected opportunity 10 years hence
Smartphones	40	130	170
Active Pharmaceutical Ingredients (API)	30	50	80
Medical devices	30	40	70
Total Opportunity 10 years hence	**100**	**220**	**320**

Source: India Herald, Customer Market Insights, Daxue Consulting, Grand View Research, Frontiers IN, Praxis Global Alliance, and Techsciresearch; All values are in US$ bn; Chinese export shift assuming a fifth of China's current exports shifts to India over the next decade; World nominal GDP growth rate of 3.5 per cent used to extrapolate the export shift for the next ten years; Indian nominal GDP growth rate of 12 per cent used to grow domestic production for the next ten years

Summary

As China's economy has been pulverized by extended Covid lockdowns, its beleaguered banking system and the country's face-off with Europe and America, India finds itself positioned to grow its share in the global market for knowledge-intensive manufactured products such as smartphones, APIs and medical devices. Cumulatively, these sectors can create a production opportunity of more than $300 bn per annum for India—i.e., enough to juice up India's GDP growth for the next decade by a whole percentage point.

8

Outsourcing 2.0: The Global Capability Centre Boom

Girls, when I was growing up, my parents used to say to me, 'Tom, finish your dinner—people in China and India are starving.' My advice to you is: Girls, finish your homework—people in China and India are starving for your jobs. And in a flat world, they can have them, because in a flat world there is no such thing as an American job. There is just a job, and in more cases than ever before it will go to the best, smartest, most productive, or cheapest worker—wherever he or she resides.

— Thomas Friedman in *The World Is Flat: A Brief History of the Twenty-First Century* (2005)

Our Wake-up Call

Since we work in the heart of India's financial capital and hence spend our lives obsessing about India's stock market, we were not aware, until a couple of years ago, of the speed at which the global capability centre (GCC) boom is sweeping across India. The authors' awakening regarding the scale of the white-collar outsourcing opportunity facing India took place in 2022 in a tier-2 city in central India. We were visiting that city to understand the scale of the post-Covid real estate boom. With that in mind, we had set up a meeting with a couple of the larger developers in that city. On a pleasant winter's morning, over plates of steaming paranthas, we sat down with these developers for a breakfast meeting. Half an hour into the meeting, one of the developers said, 'If you don't mind, can I seek your professional opinion on an important decision that I have to make?' Given how helpful this gentleman had been with his perspective on why real estate was booming in central India, we asked him to go ahead. What followed next is what makes travelling to tier-2 and tier-3 towns a central part of our job.

The developer said in Hindi: 'I have been approached by an American company I have never heard of to build an office park for them on the outskirts of our city, near the airport. The Americans want several lakhs of square feet of office space developed for them. You might say that is good news for me, but to develop that much office space I need to have confidence in the Americans. My problem is that I have never heard of this American company.'

Naturally, we asked the developer to name the company. He took out his mobile phone, peered into his emails and said in Hinglish, 'Company *ka naam hai* International Business Machines. I have not heard of them. *Aap ne inka naam suna hai kya?*'

It took us a couple of minutes to comprehend what was happening. Here was one of the world's largest IT companies contemplating a move to an Indian tier-2 city that had not hitherto been an IT hub,[1] and there we were seated in front of a local real estate developer who was worried about developing office space for IBM. Soon, however, we realized that the developer had enjoyed such a successful career building offices, villas and flats for the local residents that he had never had to look outside his home state for business. Quite understandably, then, he was oblivious of the business opportunities presented by giant Western companies beating a path to India's smaller cities in their search not just for talent but also for affordable office space in a geography where their staff would not have to endure long commutes to the office.

However, to understand how India has reached such a juncture where two sizeable new GCCs are now opening in the country every week it is worth going back in time to understand how India began its journey to become the world's back office.

From Just IT Outsourcing from India to 'Outsource Everything to India'

Throughout the 1990s and the noughties, India came to the fore as the back-end processor for all things related to IT and IT services. This happened mainly because in the new millennium, for the first time ever, transfer of information over the Internet from one corner of the world to another became super-fast and super cheap. This development opened countless opportunities for businesses across the world to spread out their operations in a cost-effective way and earn outsized profits.

India emerged as a massive beneficiary of this trend with its relatively cheap yet skilled labour being more than capable of handling IT services for global giants. According to a 2005 joint report by McKinsey and NASSCOM, India accounted for 65 per cent of the total offshore IT industry and 46 per cent of the global business process offshoring (BPO) industry.

Fast-forward two decades, and India's position as an outsourcing hub has only strengthened. More than half of the world's GCCs are in India.[2] According to NASSCOM, there are more than 1600 GCCs in India employing approximately 2 million people (expected to rise to over 4.5 million by 2030). These GCCs generate revenues to the tune of roughly Rs 4.2 lakh crores (US$ 50 billion) per annum (expected to rise up to Rs 8.4 lakh crore (US$ 110 billion) by FY30—see exhibit below).

Exhibit 8.1: GCCs are Proliferating in India

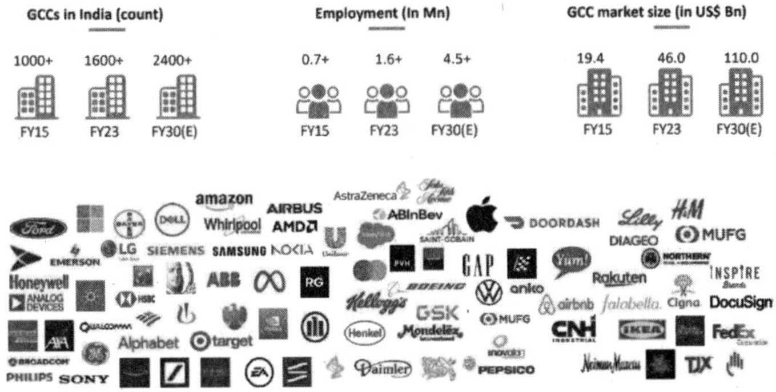

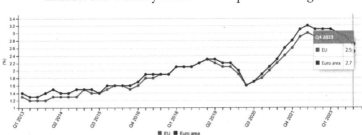

Source: ANSR Research

While all of this was happening in India, fertility rates (i.e., the number of children per women) in the West collapsed from 2 in 1990 to approximately 1.79 in 2023.[3] Consequently, Western economies are having to grapple with massive labour shortages. In particular, the structural lack of required skill sets amongst their citizens has become very evident,[4] and job vacancy rates in the Western economies are shooting up (see exhibits 2 and 3 below for Europe and exhibit 4 for America).

Exhibit 8.2: Vacancy Rates in Europe are Soaring

Source: Eurostat Job Vacancy statistics; Euro area includes the EU along with Switzerland, Norway and Iceland

Table 8.1: At a Minimum, 1 in 4 Occupations are Classified as Facing Severe Labour Shortage in Europe and are 'Outsourceable'

Occupation	No. of countries that reported employee shortage	Share of the occupations in all jobs that had a shortage of 'high severity'
Early childhood educators	12	42%
Application programmers	12	42%
Special needs teachers	11	45%
Software developers	13	38%
Systems analysts	16	25%
Software workers	12	25%

Source: EURES report on labour shortages and surpluses, 2023; underlying data taken from data submitted by EURES National Coordination Offices

More perplexingly, in the world's largest economy, the United States, many workers have chosen to not return to work post-Covid.[5] In fact, more than 44 million Americans quit their jobs in 2023. In 2024, 3.4 million quit in January alone. While the reasons for this are not entirely clear, research done by US trade bodies has shed some light on what has been labelled the 'great resignation':

> . . . in May 2022, the U.S. Chamber surveyed unemployed workers who lost their jobs during the pandemic to gain more insight into what is keeping them from returning to work. Here are a few of the key findings.

- Two-thirds (66 per cent) of Americans who lost their full-time job during the pandemic say they are only somewhat active or not very active at all in searching for a new job.
- About half (49 per cent) are not willing to take jobs that do not offer the opportunity for remote work.
- More than a quarter (26 per cent) say it will never again be essential for them to return to work.

- Nearly one in five have altered their livelihood, 17 per cent have retired, 19 per cent have transitioned to homemaker, and 14 per cent are now working part-time.
- Almost a quarter (24 per cent) say government aid packages during the pandemic have incentivized them to not actively look for work.
- Younger respondents, aged 25–34, are prioritizing personal growth over searching for a job right now; 36 per cent say they're more focused on acquiring new skills, education, or training before re-entering the job market.[6]

On the supply side, the number of employment opportunities available in America are well in excess of the number of reported unemployed people (see exhibit 4 below). This means that while Americans willing and able to work are employed, the requirement for personnel has exceeded the availability of personnel in the country.

Exhibit 8.3: For the First Time in the US in More than twenty Years, the Number of Job Openings Have Exceeded the Number of Unemployed People by a Large Magnitude

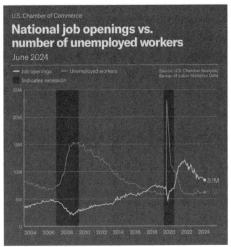

Source: US Chamber of Commerce, Bureau of Labor Statistics 2024

Moreover, the European trend relating to shortage of skilled workers is more or less true for the American economy too, with around 30 per cent of the shortage being in professional and business services, and in financial activities (see exhibit below).

Table 8.2: More than 30 per cent of the Labour Shortage in the US is in Jobs that are Easily 'Outsourceable'

Industry	Magnitude of shortage
Education and Health Services	38%
Professional and Business Services	23%
Government Workers	18%
Financial Activities	8%
Leisure and Hospitality	6%
Durable Goods Manufacturing	4%
Other Services	1%
Transportation and Utilities	1%
Information	1%
Mining and Logging	0%
Wholesale and Retail Trade	0%

Source: US Chamber of Commerce; shortage calculated as number of job openings (in thousands) minus unemployment (in thousands). Magnitude of shortage calculated as shortage in each industry divided by total shortage across industries—this measure shows the intensity of shortage in each industry; the higher the percentage the higher the intensity of shortage; data taken as of January 2024

Given the kind of jobs for which the West is facing labour shortages, and given the West's reluctance to allow large scale migration from Asia, it is but inevitable that many of these jobs will end up being outsourced to India.

An Eye-Opening Train Journey from Boston to New York City

A couple of years ago, one of us (Saurabh) took a train from Boston to New York. Although the train was advertised as an 'Express', he discovered that as in India so in America too, the express train trundled along at a leisurely pace. As a result, Saurabh had four hours to understand what the designer seated next to him was doing on her Mac PowerBook.

The lady—who was designing music systems and stereos on her PowerBook—told Saurabh that she worked for one of the world's best-known manufacturers of music stereos. She went on to say, 'While I work for the design team in Boston, all the coding work is done in Pune, India, by a really clever team of coders. These guys are so good that we have tried to convince them to migrate to America and join us in Boston. Unfortunately for us, they say they don't want to leave India. Anyhow, all the complicated stuff is done by the outsourced coding team in Pune. So, when you use our headphones or speakers you are basically buying the brilliance of the Indian coders.'

Saurabh asked the lady why she didn't hire coders locally in Boston. Her response was, 'Are you kidding me? We simply won't be able to afford talent of this quality in the United States. A coding team of this quality would cost us tens of millions of dollars for us to hire in the US, and even if we found such people and paid top dollars for them, they wouldn't hang around with us very long. On the other hand, for this top team in Pune, we are paying an Indian firm, Tata Elxsi, a few hundred thousand dollars per year per coder.'

As the American lady showed Saurabh on her laptop how she outsourced all her work to Pune and then stayed in touch with the developers using instant messaging and video-calling software, it dawned on Saurabh why more GCCs would continue to be set up in India for American and European firms. Not only is Indian talent less expensive, in most cases their level of talent is simply not available in the West at an affordable price point from the Western employer's perspective. In fact, increasingly, it is not just jobs in IT services that are being outsourced to India—everything that requires application of thought in an office environment is being outsourced to India.

Indian GCCs are now Serving a Diverse set of 'Business Critical' Functionalities

GCCs in India are currently capable of handling functionalities like HR, payroll, marketing, manufacturing, etc. (see exhibit below). While 60 per cent of the GCCs in India are focused on IT services, engineering R&D and business process management, a growing number of GCCs is focused on cutting edge work that lies on the frontiers of modern technology. An *Economic Times* report noted:

> Artificial intelligence, machine learning, advanced analytics, cybersecurity, ADAS solutions, in-vehicle infotainment, AI hardware solutions, powertrain, foundational IP solutions were some of the major focus areas for the new GCCs as well as the new centres for existing GCCs in Q4 CY2023.[7]

Table 8.3: Diversification in Verticals Served by GCCs in India is Evident in the Data for Q4 CY2023

Industry	GCC expansion in Q4 CY2023 (as a % of all GCC expansions)	Locations of expansion
Manufacturing	26%	Bengaluru, Chennai, Vadodara,
Transport and Logistics	15%	Bengaluru, Hyderabad, Chennai,
BFSI	15%	Hyderabad, Chennai
Retail/CPG	15%	Hyderabad, Ahmedabad
Hi-Tech	11%	Bengaluru, Delhi/NCR, Mumbai, Bhubaneshwar
Automotive	11%	Hyderabad, Chennai, Pune
Travel and Tourism	4%	Bengaluru
Healthcare	4%	Hyderabad

Source: ANSR Research, news articles, company press releases, social media, job boards; includes expansions set up or announced between September 2023 and January 2024

As we travel around India and speak to real estate developers (who are busy finding office space for the GCCs), bankers (who are busy building financial relationships with the GCCs and their staff) and recruiters (who are busy finding talent for the GCCs), we can see the practical implications of this surge in the GCC numbers for the Indian economy.

That being said, for a couple of decades now, a certain section in India has been criticizing GCC work as being low value-add and repetitive. The term 'cyber coolie' has been coined by these critics, who cast aspersions on GCC work to say that there is something demeaning about it. Those who hold such a point of view are now coming around to appreciating that the work done at GCCs in India is utterly central to the success of the multinational companies they serve.

Debjani Ghosh, president of NASSCOM (the trade body for the IT services industry), says that Indian GCCs are becoming 'nerve centres' of global business success. Ghosh was quoted in the press as saying in her keynote address at the NASSCOM GCC Conclave 2024 in Bengaluru: 'One of the biggest make-or-break factors for India today is to significantly increase research and development investments . . . The innovation prowess of India needs to stand out.'[8]

At the same conclave, Gunjan Samtani, head of Goldman Sachs Services India and, tellingly, the global chief operating officer of engineering at the firm, explained how the firm's GCC in India was crucial to its success in using cutting-edge tech: 'At Goldman Sachs, it took us some time to build business context and each business function. It took time to integrate the global culture of our organisation in India. Now that we are here, it is a great opportunity for us to scale up in GenAI and capitalise on leadership.'

In light of these supply-side (i.e., India has plentiful highly skilled talent thanks to 10 million graduates emerging each year from the country's vast university system[9]) and demand-side forces (i.e., the West has a massive skills shortage) at work, it is not surprising that roughly two GCCs are opening every week n India. NASSCOM says forty-seven GCCs set up in India over calendar year 2023. The *Economic Times* says that while around 20 per cent of the Forbes 2000 list of global companies had set up their GCCs in India by 2023, this share is likely to grow to 55 per cent by 2030.[10]

GCCs are Moving Beyond India's Metros

Given the infrastructure and lifestyle problems in the metropolitan cities like Bengaluru, Mumbai and the National Capital Region (e.g., long commutes, high population density, high cost of living) and given the improvements in road and airline connectivity to tier-1 and tier-2 cities, it is but natural that we are now seeing GCCs coming up in cities like Indore, Nashik, Tirunelveli and Coimbatore (see exhibit below).

The financial press in India has reported extensively on this phenomenon. For example, the *Economic Times* reported:

'From only a few tier-two locations that were attractive for GCCs earlier, India stands at a point where multiple locations offer GCCs an ecosystem of opportunities,' said Ramkumar Ramamoorthy, partner at Catalincs, and former CMD, Cognizant India.

'A place like Ahmedabad which previously saw limited technology sector interest has now become an important GCC destination for BFSI companies, thanks to the GIFT city,' he said, adding that similar interest is seen in cities such as Chandigarh, Bhubaneshwar, Nagpur, Jaipur, Lucknow and Visakhapatnam because of improved air connectivity through UDAN, availability of commercial built-to-suite real estate options, establishment of new-age private universities, and lower total cost of operations in these cities. [11]

Distinct from the growth of GCCs in the tier-2 and tier-3 cities is the preponderance of GCCs in India's 'southern seven' states, underscoring the preference of foreign investors to set up shop in those parts of the country where: (a) law and order is a given, (b) there is high availability of skilled talent and (c) physical infrastructure is in a relatively much better shape. As explained in Chapter 6, south India ticks these boxes more than any other region of the country. Indian law firm Cyril Amarchand Mangaldas's guide published for their clients on where to set up GCCs in India highlighted the steps taken by four Indian states to recognise GCCs in their statutes and provide incentives for setting up such GCCs within their state boundaries. Notably, three of the four states were southern. The law firm's guide said:

> Some states have expressly recognised GCCs under their state-level regulations and policies to incentivise Foreign Entities to set up more GCCs in their respective territories. Below is an indicative list of express call outs under state policies:
>
> Karnataka, vide its Handbook on Digital Economy Policies, Programs and Incentives, expressly recognises Bangalore as the 'destination of choice for platform engineering GCCs';
>
> Telangana, vide its ICT Policy 2021–26, commits to scaling the GCC expansion by 'strategically strengthening the ecosystem and easing the process of entry and doing business';
>
> Uttar Pradesh, vide its IT and ITeS Policy, has included GCCs within the ambit of ITeS, which allows them to claim certain fiscal benefits and non-fiscal benefits.
>
> Andhra Pradesh, vide its Industrial Development Policy 2023–27, commits to provide support to companies/ MNCs setting up a GCC. [12]

Exhibit 8.4: The Expansion of GCCs Across India has Been Across Tier-1 and Tier-2 Cities

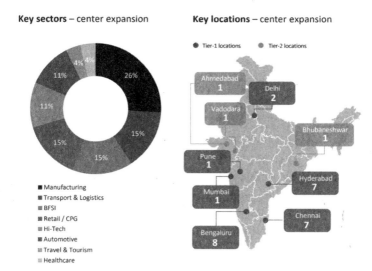

Source: ANSR research, news articles, company press release, social media, job boards

With more such GCCs being set up in smaller Indian cities, more employment opportunities are going to be created. Going by NASSCOM's estimate of around 2 million people currently work in GCCs across the country, then five years hence, if GCCs continue growing at the rate that they have (i.e., adding around 80 to their number each year), it is likely that GCCs will be employing a further 5,00,000 Indians.

Assuming that each of these jobs pays on average Rs 9 lakh ($11K) per annum, and assuming that the GCC boom sustains over the next five years, this employment boom will inject into the Indian economy an additional Rs 1 lakh crore ($11 bn) per annum, approximately, for those next five years. Applying on this the standard Keynesian fiscal multiplier of 2.3x (to account for the spillover benefits of these GCC employees' spending on leisure and consumption) suggests a benefit to the Indian economy of Rs 2–2.5 lakh crore ($25–$30 billion) per annum. That's around 1 per cent per annum of economic activity added to the Indian economy each year.

Summary

In the early years of the twenty-first century, India became the IT outsourcing hub for the Western economies. However, over the past decade, as India's talent pool has widened to sustain multiple functionalities beyond IT services; the West is also outsourcing audit, finance, HR, marketing, analytics and other functions to India. As the West's labour shortage deepens, Western firms are setting up GCCs at the rate of two every five days, thus adding to the 1600 GCCs already functioning in India. If this GCC boom sustains, then five years hence, it will create a GDP uplift for India to the tune of Rs 2.2 lakh crores ($26 billion) per annum.

Section 3

The Challengers Arrive

9

Creative Destruction on an Epic Scale

The churning of the ocean of milk, in Hindu mythology, is one of the central events in the ever-continuing struggle between the devas (gods) and the asuras (demons).

The gods . . . invited the asuras to help them recover the elixir of immortality, the amrita, from the depths of the cosmic ocean . . . In the churning of the ocean many wonderful treasures that became the prototypes for their earthly and heavenly counterparts were brought up from the depths: Chandra, the moon . . . Kamadhenu, the cow of plenty, Madira, the goddess of wine . . . Kalpavriksha, the wish-fulfilling tree . . . the goddess Lakshmi and Dhanvantari, the physician of the gods, who rose up out of the waters carrying in his hands the supreme treasure, the amrita.

–'*Sagar Manthan*', as described in the
Encyclopaedia Britannica[1]

The Pounding of Small and Medium-Sized Enterprises in India

The term 'creative destruction' was coined by Austrian economist Joseph Schumpeter in 1942. Schumpeter saw creative destruction in the innovations in the manufacturing process that increases productivity. He described it as the 'process of industrial mutation that incessantly revolutionizes the economic structure from within, incessantly destroying the old one, incessantly creating a new one'.[2]

As Schumpeter explained in his book *Capitalism, Socialism and Democracy*, the theory of creative destruction assumes that long-standing arrangements and assumptions must be destroyed to free up resources and energy to be deployed for innovation. In this mental model of how capitalism works to create a more efficient economy, economic development is the natural result of forces internal to the market and is created by the opportunities available to the people and other entities in the market to seek profit. If Schumpeter were alive, he would say that what has transpired in corporate India over the past decade is the epitome of creative destruction.

If we were to look at the data on corporate income taxes paid by Indian companies from FY12 to FY23, the latest year for which stratified income data from the Income Tax Department is available, the following points are noteworthy:

- The highest profit generators in the country, i.e., companies with average profit after tax (PAT) of Rs 1 crore (around \$1,20,000) or more have been able to grow their profits the fastest over the last decade (see exhibit below). Profit growth for such companies in the period FY12–FY23 has been at a CAGR of 13 per cent. Around 17 per cent of India's non-zero-tax-filing companies fall in this bucket, and they account for more than 98 per cent of the country's profit pie as of FY23.

- Mid-sized companies, i.e., companies with average PAT of between Rs 10 lakh and Rs 1 crore (between $12,000 to $1,20,000), have been far behind the first lot. Their profits grew at a CAGR of just 6 per cent between FY12 and FY23, implying that in real terms (i.e., after adjusting for inflation), they recorded minimal growth in profitability over the ten-year period. Around 29 per cent of India's non-zero-tax-filing companies fall in this bucket, and they account for 1.3 per cent of the country's profit pie as of FY23.

- Small companies, i.e., those generating PAT of less than Rs 10 lakh per annum (around US$12,000), have fared the worst. Their profits grew by a mere 3 per cent over FY12–FY23, implying that in real terms their profits shrank dramatically over the course of the decade (see the Appendix for more details on this). Around 54 per cent of India's non-zero-tax-filing companies fall in this bucket, and they account for 0.3 per cent of the country's profit pie as of FY23.

The underlying data used in this analysis have been sourced from the Income Tax Department of the Ministry of Finance, Government of India.[3] The Appendix provides more details from this treasure trove of data. Note that the above analysis and the following exhibit exclude the 1 million or so Indian companies which file corporate tax returns showing zero profits.

Exhibit 9.1: Companies with PAT Greater than Rs 1 Crore
(US$120,000) Have Seen Real Growth in PAT Over FY12–FY23

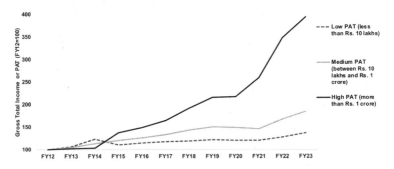

Source: Income Tax Department, Ministry of Finance; Gross total income (or
PAT) taken for each income category as per Income Tax Department data from
FY12 to FY23. For each category, YoY growth rates were calculated and then
averaged for different income categories—for low-income category, incomes
between Rs 0 to Rs 10,00,000 were considered, for medium income, Rs 10,00,001
to Rs 1,00,00,000, and for high income, more than Rs 1,00,00,001. Finally, the
average growth rates were converted to a base of 100 for FY12 to understand how
profits have progressed for companies on average

Table 9.1: Summary of India Inc.'s PAT Evolution Over FY12–FY23

Profit Bucket	Profit Threshold	Avg PAT in FY23 (Rs. Lakhs)	PAT CAGR (FY12-23)	% of India Inc's companies (as per IT filings)	% of India Inc PAT (as per IT filings)
Low PAT	Rs. 0 to Rs. 10 lakhs	2.32	3%	54%	0.3%
Medium PAT	Rs. 10 lakhs to Rs. 1 crore	36.06	6%	29%	1%
High PAT	Rs. 1 crore and above	43.02	13%	17%	98%

Source: Income Tax Department, Ministry of Finance; the penultimate column
('% of India Inc's companies') measures the percentage of non-zero tax filing
companies - i.e., excluding companies that file zero return; avg PAT calculated
as sum of all PAT under each bucket divided by the sum of number of returns
within the respective buckets

In short, the Income Tax Department data suggest that only
the most profitable 46 per cent of India's 4.65 lakh companies

which filed non-zero-tax returns in FY23 saw growth in PAT in real terms over the preceding ten years.

However, there are several limitations in using the data from the Income Tax Department, not least that over time companies are bound to move across profit buckets. So, comparing profit growth in any of the buckets over time is not an apples-to-apples comparison. For example, the list of companies in the 'high PAT' bucket (PAT of Rs 1 crore or more) in FY23 could be very different from the corresponding list in FY19. So, the fact of the soaring high-PAT bucket line could be a result of the survivorship bias inherent in the way such exercises are conducted rather than because of any genuinely strong PAT growth in the 'high PAT' bucket.

To mitigate this bias, we looked for other ways, using the most recently available data, to understand how India Inc. has fared. This search led us to a dataset provided by the Centre for Monitoring Indian Economy (CMIE), which has data on about 30,000 active companies in India on average for each of the past ten years up to FY23. By construction, therefore, the CMIE database has survivorship bias in its lowest deciles—i.e., the smaller companies who have fallen behind in profitability over the past decade are unlikely to be captured fully in the CMIE dataset. However, since this is the only time series dataset we could find on how India Inc.'s profits have evolved over the past decade, we decided to proceed with our analysis using the CMIE database.

We began by deciling these 30,000 companies into ten buckets on the basis of their PAT, with D1 containing the highest profit earners and D10 the worst loss makers. We then looked at the probability of upward movement (i.e., improvement in decile ranking; for instance, the probability of companies categorized as D8 shifting to any decile above D5).

To minimize year-to-year noise in the data, we conducted this analysis of upward movement by using rolling three-year time periods, i.e., FY13–FY16, FY14–FY17, and so on.

We found that notwithstanding the massive survivorship bias in the lower deciles (on account of many companies shuttering in the country each year),[4] the probability of upward mobility in terms of profit deciles reduced over the years secularly for most deciles. To be specific, for most deciles in the latest three-year iteration (FY20–FY23, i.e., the post-Covid period, in which the Indian economy has recovered strongly), the probability of a company in a lower decile moving into a higher decile is in the single digits (see exhibit below). As this exhibit shows, if one ignores deciles 9 and 10 (given that these are the deciles most likely to be characterized by survivorship bias), for all the other deciles, the prospect of upward mobility (in terms of a company moving into a higher profitability decile) has diminished steadily over the past decade.

Table 9.2: Probability of Upward Movement in Profit Deciles has Worsened Over the Years (Units: %)

| From | D10 | D9 | D8 | D7 | D5 | D4 | D3 | D2 |
To		>=D5			>=D4	>=D3	>=D2	=D1
FY13-16	31.4	30.3	18.1	14.4	34.5	33.8	28.9	23.9
FY14-17	32.8	34.2	17.3	13.9	31.8	31.1	27.4	20.9
FY15-18	29.1	30.8	18.3	11.3	25.5	24.5	21.1	18.0
FY16-19	30.6	30.2	16.8	10.5	23.3	21.7	17.2	13.3
FY17-20	27.0	28.7	16.1	11.9	25.5	23.8	20.9	14.1
FY18-21	30.7	28.3	14.1	10.2	25.0	25.7	21.2	13.5
FY19-22	34.5	28.3	11.6	8.8	20.2	19.1	16.5	11.6
FY20-23	39.3	28.3	8.4	5.6	9.0	7.8	5.8	3.9

Source: CMIE Prowess (sourced from IIFL Capital); underlying companies as of FY23; due to unavailability of point-in-time data going as far back as FY13, these same companies' PAT data was sourced for the last ten years; the probabilities of each transition matrix for each of the three-years period was calculated separately and the probabilities of the respective decile of companies moving upwards were then summed accordingly; each entry in the table represents such summed probabilities

Dawn of a New, more Schumpeterian Era for India Inc.

So far in this chapter, we have highlighted—using data from the Income Tax Department—the much faster growth that companies with PAT greater than Rs 1 crore have been able to register, compared with the rest of the corporate population in India. Furthermore, the CMIE data, when crunched, has shown that upward mobility in the corporate sector has diminished in the past decade.

However, there is a silver lining in this. As can be seen in the exhibit below, in the post-Covid world, as data from the CMIE shows, the profit share of the twenty most profitable companies in India (expressed as a share of the profits generated by more or less the entirety of India's corporate community) has dropped from more than 100 per cent to 40 per cent, implying that smaller companies have successfully pulled away profits from the top twenty giants of India Inc. This raises two questions:

1. Does the CMIE data corroborate this finding of smaller companies doing better in post-Covid India?
2. Why are smaller companies doing better in terms of demonstrating upward mobility in profitability in post-Covid India?

The rest of this chapter is focused on answering these two questions.

Exhibit 9.2: PAT Concentration of the top 20 Companies (Ranked by PAT) has Diminished Post-Covid

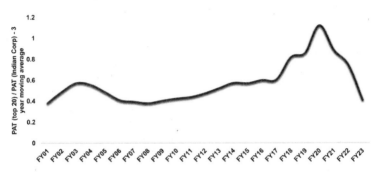

Source: CMIE (sourced by IIFL Capital), Bloomberg, Ace Equity; the CMIE data for FY23 pertains to nearly 14,000 companies whose data have been updated, as opposed to data for the previous years, which covered nearly 30,000 companies. PAT, for the top 20 has been checked for companies as of each of the financial years; due to high variance in the measure, a three-year average has been calculated to smoothen out any sudden movements

To answer the first question, we conducted a final layer of analysis. We looked at companies at intervals of three years and kept the deciles basis PAT constant for those three years. This essentially means that corporate mobility across PAT deciles was *not* considered within the three-year period. So, for example, if a company is in decile 7 at the beginning of the three-year period, then, even though by the third year the company might in fact have moved to a higher (or lower) decile, it is tagged as a 'decile 7' company for the entirety of the three-year crunch.

This analysis showed that Decile 2 companies—i.e., the companies one rung below the most profitable decile— have performed the best in terms of profit growth (see exhibit below). This observation derived from the CMIE data squares nicely with what we find in the Income Tax Department data, namely, that it is the not the 900 largest companies in India which are growing profits the fastest. Instead, it is the 6000 companies below the 'rulers' that have shown the fastest growth in corporate profitability over the past decade. In fact, it is the rise of the 6000 companies below the 900 largest companies which is resulting in the profit-concentration curve in Figure 9.4 dipping downwards in the post-Covid era.

Exhibit 9.3: Decile 2 on Average Does the Best in Terms of PAT Compounding Over the Years When Mobility is Not Considered

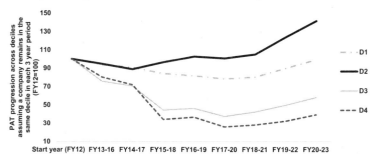

Source: CMIE Prowess (sourced from IIFL Capital); underlying companies as of FY23; due to unavailability of point-in-time data going as far back as FY13, the PAT data for these companies were sourced for the last ten years; a company classified under a particular decile was kept constant in that decile for the next 3 years and its profit CAGR was averaged across deciles; only deciles 1 to 4 have been considered because of inconsistency in CAGR availability for the deciles beyond that owing to negative profits (losses)

The above exhibit shows that in a development that would have delighted Joseph Schumpeter, the most efficient smaller companies appear to be ascending towards the higher PAT deciles. On the other hand, more than 80 per cent of the smaller companies are being left behind as the Indian economy becomes larger, more efficient and more competitive. That leads us to the question of what is going on in the underlying economy to create these starkly divergent trends. Specifically, what is underpinning the rise of Decile 2—a category we have dubbed as the 'Challengers'—in the post-FY15 period.

Opportunities for the Best and Stress for the Rest

Imagine a village economy cut off from the rest of the world with no road or telecom connectivity to anywhere. In such a village, a range of smaller business, such as the barber, the greengrocer, the butcher, the blacksmith, the moneylender, etc., will build profitable local monopolies.

Now imagine that one fine day this village gets road and telephone connectivity to the nearest large city, which is ten kilometres away. Here is what is likely to happen now:

1. The most profitable and most enterprising companies in the village will set up branch operations in the large city, and if they prosper there, repatriate some of their profits back to the native village to scale up their village enterprise, thereby grabbing profit share in their native village.
2. Aggressive companies from the large city will enter the village and offer lower prices alongside better products to the villagers. This will lead to many of the village enterprises shutting down as they will not have the technology, the expertise and the scale of the big-city competitors.
3. Over time, the number of companies in the village will shrink, both because of consolidation in each sector in the village as the smaller village enterprises struggle to survive, and also because of imports of many necessities coming from the big city.

In very simple terms, this is what has happened in India over the past decade. The nation has gone from being a village-like economy (with poor connectivity between various regions in the country) to big-city integration with the village (or invasion of the village, depending your point of view) as connectivity improved. On the bigger, pan-India canvas in the aftermath of this integration, more efficient companies have grabbed profit share and, in doing so, have pulled down profits for their less efficient competitors.

As we have described in the preceding chapters, the joining up of India took place digitally (through the advent of Jan Dhan bank accounts, Aadhaar, Jio, UPI and the India Stack), which in turn made accessibility to the markets, payment systems and information less asymmetric. Post-2017, this intertwined with GST and the doubling of the national highway network to deliver a transformational change in the economic landscape, one which a few companies (the largest 7000 companies in the country, most of whom are 'Challengers') were able to seize but most were overwhelmed by.[5]

Three Effects that Drove the Rise in Democratization of Profits

The improvement in the fortunes of the small yet efficient Challenger companies has been a relatively recent phenomenon, having emerged over the past decade. As with any economic reform, it takes time before the impact of the fruits of change begin showing in the broader economy. We reckon that this has started happening, especially in the post-Covid era when the turbulence created by economic reforms (the banking sector clean-up in 2015–17, the GST implementation in 2017 and so on) has largely dissipated, paving the way for a golden era for efficient, smaller companies. More specifically, three distinct effects that have emerged in the last decade have ushered in this new era of increased efficiency for smaller companies (the 'Challengers') and rising competition for large companies (the 'Rulers').

Effect #1: The Fall of the Tax-Evading and Inefficient Small Companies

With the banking system clean-up triggered by the then RBI governor Raghuram Rajan in 2015 via the Asset Quality Review, followed by the introduction of the Insolvency and Bankruptcy Code (IBC) in 2017 and the implementation of GST in 2017, many small tax-evading companies saw their profits disappear. The adverse situation they found themselves in was further exacerbated by the Covid-related lockdowns and disruptions. This cocktail of adversities hammered the bottom 50 per cent of the 'Plebians'—see the bottom right quadrant in the exhibit below.

This clean-up of the system was brutal and yet essential for the dawn of an era where the next effect could start to play out.

Effect #2: The Rise of Nimble and Efficient Smaller Companies

As the country's inefficient smaller companies were battered by the structural economic reforms, a new breed of companies within this cohort not only survived this pounding but also emerged in the post-Covid world with sparkling growth in profits. These companies—the 6000 'Challengers' in our analysis with profit after tax ranging from Rs 50 crore to Rs 500 crore (US\$6mn–US\$60mn)—invested in modern technology, went online, embraced UPI and the India Stack, improved their efficiency and product quality and became highly profitable in the new and increasingly formalized Indian economy.

This robust effect #2, we reckon, is a precursor to the larger effect #3, which could prove to be transformational over the coming years.

Effect #3: Challenging of the Existing Rulers

As the small, fast-growing, efficient 'Challengers' expand, they are creating intense competition for their larger competitors, the 'Rulers', i.e., companies with PAT in excess of Rs 500 crore ($60mn). In the years to come, the smaller 'Challengers', with their superior business models and greater operational efficiencies, are likely to contest the 'Rulers' and seek to grab significant profit share from them.

We summarize the three effects using a 2x2 matrix (see the exhibit below), where on one axis we have the size of companies (large or small) and on the other their nature of business (organized or unorganized). Most Indian companies sit in the bottom right quadrant and have witnessed stagnation in their profits over the past decade (effect #1). The most efficient and enterprising smaller companies have shifted over the past decade, and especially post-Covid, from the bottom right to the bottom left quadrant (effect #2).

The next step will be a shift of the fittest smaller companies from the bottom left to the top left quadrant (effect #3). We now turn to two cases studies that help contextualize the manner in which these effects are playing out in contemporary India.

Table 9.3: Corporate Profits in the Indian Economy are Shifting From the Bottom Right to the Bottom Left Quadrant

	Organized Companies	Unorganized Companies
Large Companies	**'Rulers'**: There are 900+ companies (0.2% of all profitable companies) in this quadrant. These are: 1. Large, dominant, highly profitable companies (with PAT of more than Rs 500cr ($60mn) which have built market-leading pan-India franchises. 2. With their extensive distribution reach (capitalizing on India's infra build-out), automated manufacturing and large scale of operations (capitalizing on UPI & the India Stack), they have made it very hard for small companies to compete with them. 62% of India's profits sit in this quadrant. Their FY12–FY23 PAT CAGR is 15%.	No such companies exist today but until a decade ago this was a significant part of the Indian economy e.g., the $10bn liquor empire run by Ponty Chadha[i].
Small Companies	**'Challengers'**: 1–1.5% of India's companies by count (6,000) sit in this quadrant. These firms: 1. Are tax-paying smaller companies who have used the structural changes in the economy (GST, Jio, India Stack, infra build-out) to their benefit. 2. Are earning PAT of between Rs 50 crores to Rs 500 crores ($6mn–60mn). 3. Have seen an upswing in their fortunes since the end of the pandemic. Around 22% of India's profits sits in this quadrant. Their FY12–FY23 PAT CAGR is 15%.	**'Plebians'**: Around 99% of India's companies by count sit in this quadrant. 44% of them have been able to grow PAT in real terms between FY12 and FY23. 1. These companies were hammered by the formalization of the economy and thus lost their main competitive advantage, which was tax evasion. 2. These companies struggled to adopt modern IT systems, could not hire talent and thus could not benefit from GST, mobile broadband and UPI. 3. Many of these companies have shrunk or seen their profits fall sharply. 16% of India's profits sits in this quadrant. Their FY12–FY23 PAT CAGR is a mere 6%.

Source: Income Tax Department data.

Case study #1

The 'Challenger' Ecosystem—Tamil Nadu—a Microcosm of Modern India's Changing Fortunes

Roughly 500 km south-west of Chennai is the thriving city of Coimbatore. It is large enough to be called a city, yet not large enough to be a tier-1 city. What distinguishes Coimbatore from the major cities in north India are its thriving industries ranging from spinning mills to engineering goods (from castings, textile machinery and auto-components to pump sets and wet grinders). Started by the local Kammavar Naidus who migrated to Coimbatore from Andhra Pradesh, these industries have become entrenched in Coimbatore's fabric, making the city a buzzing hub of entrepreneurial and industrial activity. In fact, the Kammavar Naidus own companies like Suguna Foods, Elgi Equipment and Lakshmi Machine Works—names that resonate not just within Tamil Nadu but pan-India.

However, what is even more interesting is that Coimbatore isn't the only such city or town in the state of Tamil Nadu that showcases entrenched entrepreneurial values and, as a result, thriving industries. The nearby towns of Tiruppur, Erode, Salem, Namakkal, Karur and others also have industries and small capitalist clusters of the Kongu Vellalar, or Gounder, community.

Successful small-and-medium-sized businesses (of the bottom left quadrant variety), as opposed to the colossal conglomerates (in the top left quadrant) found in Mumbai, have become the mainstay of the economy in Tamil Nadu. As a result, the contributors to gross valued added (GVA) for Tamil Nadu are more broad-based and diversified than in the rest of India. For instance, GVA from industry contributes roughly 23 per cent to Tamil Nadu's total GVA while employing 18 per cent of the total workforce of the state. The same figures for India as a whole are 19 per cent and 12 per cent, respectively.[6]

Case study #2 – A 'Challenger' Company:

A Start-Up in Suburban Mumbai Which Moved From the Bottom Right to the Bottom Left Quadrant

The rise of this small company situated in the semi-industrial Mumbai suburb of Andheri is emblematic of the changes that are sweeping across India. Founded in 2018 with a paid-up capital of Rs 8 crore ($1 mn), this company focused on providing portfolio management services to affluent Indian families spread across India's metros and tier-1 and tier-2 cities. With over 400 companies operating in this space in India, this start-up had its work cut out for it, given that it takes decades to build a brand and a good reputation amongst affluent Indian families, who form the core customer base for the portfolio management industry.

The company made a loss of Rs 1.5 crore in its first year of operations. But cut to the present day, and as of FY24 this firm has assets under management of Rs 7000 crores (US$ 0.9 billion) and PAT of Rs 30 crore (US$4 million). The name of the start-up, as many of you would have guessed, is Marcellus Investment Managers, a company founded with its shareholders' lifetime savings. Sustained investments in talent (rank-holding chartered accountants and engineers, and award-winning analysts), in state-of-the-art technologies (Salesforce for customer relationship management, WealthSpectrum for fund operations, Bloomberg for trading) and in intellectual property (bestselling books, proprietary forensic databases, proprietary investment techniques) helped Marcellus overcome formidable challenges and go from losses in its first couple of years to strong profitability from its third year onwards. It is this combination of knowhow combined with access to equity capital that hundreds of thousands of small businesses in India need to shift from the bottom right to the bottom right left quadrant in the preceding exhibit.

Summary

Crunching data from the Income Tax Department, one finds that among Indian companies that filed non-zero-tax returns for FY23, only 46 per cent saw growth in PAT in real terms over the preceding ten years. And this 46 per cent accounted for 99.7 per cent of corporate India's PAT. Further, data from the CMIE show that the prospect of upward mobility (in terms of companies moving from a lower-profit decile into a higher-profit decile) has diminished steadily over the past decade. However, both datasets show that the fastest-growing profit generators in India are not from among the top 900 companies; instead, they are from among the 6000 companies below the top 900. They grew profits the fastest between FY12 and FY23. As the Indian economy stabilizes after successive reform-related and external shocks, these 'Challenger' companies are the ones that seem to have adapted most efficiently to the new realities of a networked, consolidated, formalized and competitive free-market economy.

Epilogue

Back to Bengaluru to Witness the Dawn of a New Era

After the reforms and redirection of technological change in the second half of the nineteenth century, a degree of hope seemed warranted. For the first time in thousands of years, there was a confluence of rapid technological progress and institutional preconditions for the benefits to be shared beyond a narrow elite.

—Daron Acemoglu and Simon Johnson in *Power and Progress: Our Thousand Year Struggle over Technology and Prosperity*, 2023

Figure 1: Broad-Based Technological Shifts in the US Predate Its Economic Growth in the twentieth Century

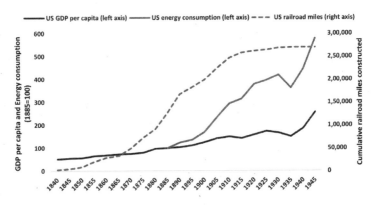

Source: Bolt and van Zanden—Maddison database 2023, National Bureau of Economic Research sourced from Federal Reserve of St Louis, US Energy Information Administration; GDP per capita figures taken from Maddison database and based on 2011 international $ prices; electricity consumption is estimated primary energy consumption in quadrillion BTU; both GDP per capita and energy consumption are normalized to 1885=100 for comparison purposes; railroad miles data from St Louis Fed converted to cumulative beginning 1830 and reported in miles

Introduction

We began this book by describing how two nondescript villages on the outskirts of Bangalore were transformed by the economic liberalization of 1991. It is only appropriate, therefore, that we end this book in the same city, now called Bengaluru, and in the thriving neighbourhood of Koramangala. That's where, on a steaming hot summer's day in 2024, we got an early glimpse of how artificial intelligence (AI) can change the lives of India's 1.4 billion denizens for the better.

The rise of America in the twentieth century demonstrated that enabling infrastructure (railroads, electricity, telegraph, etc.), which lowers the cost of transport and communication, tends to precede economic growth—see the opening exhibit of this chapter. In contemporary India, as is well understood now, the methodical building of each layer of the India Stack to leverage technology as a public good (the so-called 'digital public goods') has been tremendously successful.

The JAM trinity (Jan Dhan, Aadhaar and the mobile phone) has essentially pulled the country into the digital realm by giving each citizen an identity (using Aadhaar), access to financial means (using Jan Dhan bank accounts) and overall access to the Internet. The joining of all of this together seems to have created a robust ecosystem that facilitates democratization of information and costless access to the financial system.

Built on top of this is the unified payments interface (or UPI) that facilitates transactions seamlessly and instantaneously across bank accounts (with no transaction costs at all for the payer or the receiver). After growing exponentially through the Covid pandemic, UPI transactions crossed Rs 180 trillion (or approximately US$ 2.17 trillion per annum) as of December 2023. This constitutes more than 50 per cent of the Indian GDP! This rapid spread of a low-cost, easy-to-use digital payments system has conferred many benefits on SMEs and MSMEs, including: (1) reduction in the time taken to settle transactions and, as a result, reduction in working capital cycles; and (2) elimination of the transaction costs associated with payments by plastic card, cheque (which entailed visits to the bank) and cash (which too could entail visits to the bank and/or physical travel to take or make payments).

Figure 2: The Boom in UPI Transactions (Value and Volume) is Testimony to Successful Digitalization in the Indian Economy

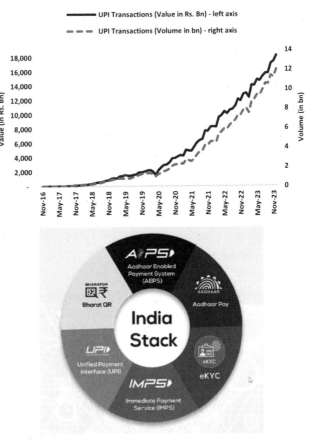

Interestingly, while technology in the form of the India Stack has had a transformative impact on the Indian economy, two large constituencies have not yet been able to experience its full benefits—the roughly 26 per cent of the Indian population that is illiterate[1] (as of 2022), and the 47.6 per cent of the people in India who do not have access to Internet[2] (as of 2024).

In fact, the literacy rate of 74 per cent indicates literacy in any language i.e., people can be literate in their mother tongues and not necessarily in English. This becomes a real obstacle to digitization in India as most web applications and data on the Internet are developed in the English language, which may serve the purpose for people living in English-speaking countries but doesn't go very far in a country as diverse as India, where the language and dialect change every kilometre and where only 10.6 per cent of the population is proficient in the use of English.[3]

As the mode of Internet access increasingly consists of voice-powered bots using natural language processing, the need for adaption of the India Stack grows. Secondly, as the use of AI to enhance functionality and improve user experience becomes widespread, various types of opportunities open up to take the India Stack to the next level.

India Stack 2.0: Application of AI to the India Stack

The development of AI in both America and China has been characterized by large tech companies spending billions of dollars in training their bots to solve problems for which users are willing to pay a fee. This 'privatization' of AI for corporate profit is a necessary engine for the further development of this nascent technology.

However, what this also means is that AI, as developed in the West, seems unlikely to address the needs of the majority of Indians who are:

(a) not going to be in a position to be able to afford to pay for AI; and
(b) likely to have use cases which the West will not— for example, a Tamil-speaking farmer seeking to identify which of the hundreds of Central and

state government schemes, subsidies and loans she's
eligible for; or an Assamese-speaking eighteen-
year old girl from a scheduled tribe in a village near
Digboi seeking to figure out which government or
private-sector scholarship can help her pay her way
through university.

Delving deeper into the use cases where AI could help India,
it becomes obvious that the Western training data fed into
Western AI tools like ChatGPT will make them relevant
only to that section of the Indian economy whose problems
are similar to that of the West, such as a financial analyst in
the Indian stock market trying to synthesize learnings from the
last twenty years of published financial data, annual reports and
conference-call transcripts of a listed company in the country,
or an executive seeking to book a camping holiday for four in
the Himalayas.

To harness the power of AI for use cases that are more unique
to India, EkStep Foundation, co-founded by Nandan Nilekani,
Rohini Nilekani and Shankar Maruwada in Bengaluru, is using
the tech prowess of its volunteers, who are also stalwarts in their
respective fields, to build an AI stack that can be labelled as
India Stack 2.0.

To that end, EkStep has funded a lab in IIT Madras called
AI4Bharat, which, among other things, has been responsible
for building an open stack in AI, comprising high-quality data,
models and tools around Indic languages. AI4Bharat is the digital
public good powering India's National Language Translation
Mission, or Bhashini, which is a digital public infrastructure
(DPI) providing language translation AI technology as a
service to many government initiatives. Bhashini currently
boasts proficiency in eleven Indian languages in speech form
and twenty-two in text form.[4] This is the first and arguably

the most crucial step in making cutting-edge technology accessible to all.

It is important to note here that the Western tech giants, Google and Microsoft, also have AI initiatives built around India's vernacular languages. However, given that these are listed for-profit enterprises, it is not obvious to what extent they will harness AI for use cases central to India's economic development. Furthermore, given their priorities, it is not clear what case exists for them to create something that would address the need for social development in the country. The limited role of the Western tech giants in creating India Stack 1.0 suggests that they are likely to remain marginal players as India's best brains work on creating India Stack 2.0.

An indigenous AI module for India with a Few Remarkable Advantages

Made-in-India AI solutions are targeted at specific issues, the resolution of which is central to India's development. These solutions have the capacity to drive meaningful change by being:

- Use-case Specific, where distinct issues specific to India can be addressed and resolved. For instance, if the government wishes to understand how effective a particular scheme like MNREGA has been in a particular state, such as Madhya Pradesh (or a particular district in Madhya Pradesh), government officials should be able to create a voice-operated bot that will not only record responses from lakhs of people but also analyse and synthesize the data to help draw actionable insights.

- More Inclusive, so that everyone can benefit regardless of which strata of society they belong to and which language they speak. Bhashini's development is crucial here for overcoming the English language hurdle that the Internet currently poses for the majority of Indians. The 'affordability' issue around AI is the second leg of the inclusivity challenge that the team at EkStep is working on.

- Easier to Build into Powerful New Applications, so that the building blocks of the solutions will be available to all (on an 'open source' basis), to be leveraged free of cost and when needed. Sunbird (sunbird.org[5]) is one such digital public good; it creates the building blocks of code that anyone can use to create solutions to address the issue or use case they are targeting. For instance, the QR code on the Cowin vaccine certificate came from a block of code on Sunbird.

Figure 3: Building Blocks on Sunbird were Used to Generate the QR Codes on Covid Vaccine Certificates

Source: Sunbird.org, CoWin; Copyrights of above images are reserved with its creator and their usage here is for illustration purposes only

These three advantages make indigenous application of AI to the India Stack an economic necessity.

The Initiatives Already Underway

Several teams at EkStep along with IIT Madras, Bhashini, several Government departments, startups and big tech players have already begun working on digital public goods (DPGs) that marry AI with the India Stack. Summarized below are three DPGs that we reckon could have a transformative social and economic impact in the country:

- The 'Jan Ki Baat' Idea: 'People plus AI', the team behind the Jan Ki Baat idea, defines it as a game changer, which can truly touch the lives of people and make an impact by listening to them, understanding their concerns, synthesizing information and generating actionable insights for organizations that cater to very large populations (such as the government of India). [6]

  The traditional bots currently in use answer questions asked by users (think of the chatbots available on the apps or websites of private-sector banks). Jan Ki Baat reverses this paradigm by asking targeted questions to people, eliciting responses from them from conversations—a bot talks to you as if there is a human being at the other end of the line wishing to understand the issues you face or what you find really helpful, let's say, when applying for a home loan under the PM Awas Yojana. This shift in paradigm helps the bot get more information—not just from what is spoken, but also from the tonality of the speaker, his or her emotions (like anger at or happiness with the service provided) and other non-verbal cues. This is right now at a demo stage. The People plus AI team believes this bot and the general Jan Ki Baat idea can revolutionize government assessment of the success of its schemes and enhance them using the on-ground feedback it gets at a population scale. For the corporate sector, such a concept can be used to launch products, collect customer feedback at speed and help corporations adapt their launch plans (or their products) accordingly.

- e-Jaadui Pitara (See More Here): The government of India has, through the years, launched innumerable schemes to improve the education system. Given the practical difficulties of implementation, these plans often stay on paper and get filed away in some corner in some government office, never to be looked at again. One such recent policy that was introduced was the Jaadui Pitara, or 'magic box', by the National Council of Educational Research and Training (NCERT) as part of the implementation of the National Education Policy (NEP). It is an actual box filled with puzzles, games and toys aimed at imparting education in the spirit of 'learn and play'. This box turned out to weigh 11 kg and cost over Rs 10,000, making it financially and logistically impossible to be procured and shipped to all the government-run schools in the country.[7]

Inspired by this, the EkStep Foundation partnered with NCERT and the education ministry to come up with a digital solution in the form of e-Jaadui Pitara, an app and a bot (which can be used on WhatsApp) to help make the process of learning fun and easy for all. The bot currently has three modules, called Teacher Tara, Parent Tara and Katha Sakhee, each targeting a specific need and demography.

For example, if a teacher sitting in a village in the Latur district of Maharashtra wishes to know how she can incorporate play into her lesson for her students, some of whom are visually challenged, she can ask the Teacher Tara bot for help (by typing in her request or by speaking to it) in eleven different languages. The bot will promptly refer to the existing official and authoritative material on the subject, come up with an actionable way of incorporating play for visually challenged students and will also provide the teacher reference to the relevant source material. Similarly, both parents and teachers can use Katha Sakhee to generate stories for their children by just providing the bot a few character references and morals they wish to instill in their children, using which the bot module will structure one for them.

The bot is built using the Open AI stack of AI4Bharat, Bhashini and Sunbird AI Assistant, and leverages the existing national-scale digital infrastructure of DIKSHA (diksha.gov.in). The availability of this open AI stack means that the bot can also be repurposed by companies to give their consumers actionable solutions for product installation or their tech support-related problems (for example, instructions for self-installation of a water purifier).

- Open Network for Education and Skilling Transformation (ONEST): The issue of unavailability of information for students seeking to undertake skilling courses or to apply for apprenticeships and scholarships is one that most of us at Marcellus have lived through in our teenage years. So is the problem on the supply side, with employers being unable to reach out to talent all across the country, whether to support it using their CSR funds or to recruit it. ONEST solves this problem to some extent by connecting siloed platforms by means of an open network. Utilizing the same tech architecture as the Open Network for Digital Commerce (ONDC), the network of ONEST connects the demand and the supply sides with each other. [8]

On ONEST, a biotech student in a remote village in Uttar Pradesh can undertake courses relevant to her field to further enhance her skill sets. Once she completes them, she gets a digitally verifiable credential, which can be stored on her ID (her identity is verified via Aadhaar and PAN). An employer in Mumbai seeking to recruit a biotechnologist can use ONEST and find on the network the best student who has aced a practical course. If the employer is also seeking to support students in whom it sees potential with its CSR funds, it can find them through ONEST and easily keep track of them, no matter where in the country the beneficiaries reside. This has the potential to democratize access to opportunities and address the permanently pertinent issue of demand-supply mismatch in the labour market.

These three initiatives do not constitute an exhaustive list when it comes to leveraging AI to enhance the India Stack, thereby producing transformative DPGs. India's brightest brains are working on more such initiatives to democratize the citizenry's access to affordable modern technology, which can improve social and economic outcomes.

India-Specific AI is not Without its Limitations

Even as it becomes increasingly evident that application of AI to solve India's problems holds great promise to transform economic and social outcomes, the challenges of using AI in India are also coming to the fore.

- There is a Marginal Cost to Using AI: While the marginal cost of providing a service to an additional person over the Internet is close to zero, the marginal cost of providing AI-based solutions is not zero. To be specific, the marginal cost of AI is the GPU burn— or in simple terms, the cost of providing computing capacity every single time AI is used. This makes wide-scale implementation of AI-driven modules a little trickier than implementing modules under India Stack 1.0, leaving a very tough question lingering—who will pay for this technology? To be specific, when an Odiya farmer earning a living that keeps him just above the poverty line uses AI to identify which subsidy or loan he's eligible for, who will pay for the GPU burn is something that needs to be worked out.

- Ground-Up Development of Use Cases: Because India is at a very different stage of economic development relative to the West or relative to its developing peers, the use cases required to tailor AI-based solutions will need to be created from scratch. Much of the training data might also have to be created from a zero (or near-zero) base. The critical use cases that merit application of AI, and the key stakeholders, beneficiaries and service providers, will need to be identified. Training data will have to be collected, and then, once the bots are implemented to address the India-specific use cases, ongoing surveillance will have to be put in place to prevent both 'hallucinations' (where AI models start observing non-existent patterns, or patterns that are imperceptible to humans in data, often leading to nonsensical results) and misuse of the installed apparatus.

- Need to Collect and Train Vast Amounts of Data: Because of the unique characteristics of a country like India (where language, dialect, sensibility and even behaviour in similar situations keep changing with geography), much of the training data will have to be collected from the real world rather than picked up from already available data on the web. This is also because the available data currently does not capture everything, especially when it comes to those problems that require the most urgent remediation. For instance, there would hardly be any data on which fertilizer is to be used for a particular crop, let's say, bajra, in a small hamlet of a district in Bihar, in the regional dialect that is understood by the people and the farmers living there.

Summary

India Stack 1.0 has already democratized the citizenry's access to markets. India Stack 2.0 can further this process, effectively reducing the gap between small and large companies when it comes to use of technology to build competitive advantages. That, in turn, could make the economy more competitive and improve India's chances—especially for its smaller firms—to build businesses which can compete successfully in the global market. Beyond IT services and pharmaceuticals, India has struggled to build an export economy capable of competing on the world stage. India Stack 2.0, if built and executed at population-wide scale, promises to help India build competitive advantages at the economy-wide level.

Acknowledgements

While both authors have studied economics at the postgraduate level, neither of us is a practising economist, our day job being to invest the monies of Indian families and foreign institutional investors in the Indian stock market. So, two years ago, it was with a degree of trepidation that we discussed with Penguin Random House's Milee Ashwarya and Manish Kumar our idea of a book on how India is changing. Milee and Manish's enthusiastic support for our idea did much to energize us as we wrote this book over the course of 2023 and 2024. We thank them for their practical and intellectual support in executing this book.

Several of the ideas in this book arose during our discussions with other investors, entrepreneurs, policymakers, academics and journalists. We have learnt much from talking to and reading material written by Aditi Phadnis, A.K. Bhattacharya, Alex Travelli, Anirudha Dutta, Anshuman Tiwari, Anupam Gupta, Ashish Dhawan, Ashok Gulati, Ashwini Deshpande, Devangshu Datta, Dharmendra Singh Gangwar, Durgesh Shah, Gaurav Gupta, Govinda Rao, Gurcharan Das, Harish Damodaran, Harsh Mariwala, Ila Patnaik, Jairam Ramesh, John Kay, Josh Felman, Latha Venkatesh, Manish Sabharwal, M.K. Venu, Monika Halan, Montek Singh Ahluwalia, M.R. Madhavan, Mridula Ramesh, N. Mahalakshmi, Narotam Sekhsaria, Neeraj Choksi, Nemish Shah, Niranjan Rajadhyaksha, Nrupesh Shah, Pavan Ahluwalia, Patrick Foulis,

Pramit Bhattacharya, Pramod Varma, Pronab Sen, Rathin Roy, Rajdeep Sardesai, Rajeev Mantri, Rajen Mariwala, Rohit Rajendran, Sanjoy Bhattacharyya, Santosh Nair, Shamika Ravi, Shankar Maruwada, Shankkar Aiyar, Shailendra Bhatnagar, Shekhar Gupta, Siddharth Shetty, Sudipto Mundle, Sujith Nair, Sumit Ghorawat, Surabhi Upadhyay, Swapan Dasgupta, Tanuj Bhojwani, T.N. Ninan, T.C.A. Anant, Thomas Easton, T.V. Mohandas Pai, T.V. Somanathan, Tripti Lahiri, V. Anantha Nageswaran, and Vinay Sitapati. We are grateful to these giants for allowing us to stand on their broad shoulders.

Several of the current and former executives, promoters and board members of Marcellus's investee companies also played a key role in triggering chains of thought which culminated in some of the ideas contained in this book. We thank Anup Bagchi, Balram Yadav, Bhargav Dasgupta, Bhaskar Bhat, C.K. Venkataram, Dipak Gupta, Gaurang Shah, Harish Bhat, Jalaj Dani, Kitty Agarwal, Manish Choksi, Nandan Nilekani, Nilesh Mundra, Pirojsha Godrej, Raamdeo Agarwal, Rafique Malik, Rajesh Rai, Sandeep Bakhshi, Sanjeev Bikhchandani, Sashidhar Jagdishan and Vellayan Subbiah.

Our colleague, Salil Desai, read the early drafts of all the chapters in this book and helped us refine the structuring of the chapters. The authors are very thankful to Salil for his steady flow of inputs for this book.

Another colleague, Naren VP, was on hand to guide the two Mumbai-based authors through the extensive suburbs of the megapolis that is now Bangalore. Without Naren's help, the Prologue and Epilogue of this book would have lacked colour and detail.

The authors would like to thank Jeet Mukherjea for his help in pulling together the 'Further Reading' section of the book. Kripa Ramachandran's superb copy editing and Neeraj Nath's stunning cover design have added enormous value to the quality of the book and the authors are grateful to both of these professionals from Penguin Random House.

Saurabh would like to thank his co-author Nandita Rajhansa for not only balancing the analytical load of her day job and her Chartered Financial Analyst (CFA) exam with her workload for this book but also for her persistence in tracking down elusive datasets and then teasing out of them layers of actionable investment insights. Nandita's ability to take megabytes of data and distil them into a couple of killer exhibits has added the much needed 'quantification' to the qualitative insights Saurabh seeks out from his research trips to various parts of India.

For a decade, Saurabh worked with and travelled around the world with Ritika Mankar and Sumit Shekhar. Saurabh is thankful to these bright young economists for never-ending debates—usually on planes, trains and automobiles—on how the Indian economy works. Saurabh owes his mental models of how India works to those protracted debates because applied economics is learnt on the field and not in the classroom.

Saurabh is very grateful to his wife Sarbani and the two teenagers who dominate Sarbani and Saurabh's lives, Jeet and Malini, for bearing with him while he juggled his responsibilities at Marcellus with the workload resulting from his co-authorship of this book.

Nandita would like to thank her parents, Chetan and Dhanashree Rajhansa, for being resolute pillars of support throughout her life, and especially during the time she juggled multiple roles at work and at home. Without their encouragement and push, a lot of the work that went into this book would not have been possible. Equally pivotal has been the role of her extended family (her grandmother Poornima, aunt Vandana and cousin Mihir) in Mumbai, who have ensured that she eats on time and has enough time and space to dedicate to the multiple tasks that she had to attend to. She is also grateful for the support and understanding provided by her colleagues at Marcellus and her friends, which have been invaluable and at times critical for helping her push the pedal and fire on all engines. And Sakshi Sohoni, friend and classmate from university, has been the one person whom Nandita could turn to in order to understand the intricacies and vagaries of everything under the sun.

Appendix

Midpoint of PAT buckets	FY12	FY13	FY14	FY15	FY16	FY17	FY18	FY19	FY20	FY21	FY22	FY23	PAT category	PAT bucket average	FY12-23 CAGR
75K	100	107	126	109	113	117	117	117	117	118	122	126	Low PAT	137	3%
1.75 lakhs	100	109	148	106	108	109	110	110	110	112	117	124			
2.25 lakhs	100	109	138	110	115	117	116	117	117	121	122	133			
3 lakhs	100	106	123	111	114	118	117	118	118	116	121	134			
3.75 lakhs	100	103	118	111	115	118	124	120	125	124	127	137			
4.25 lakhs	100	105	119	112	117	119	124	124	122	122	133	141			
4.75 lakhs	100	104	119	108	116	119	120	124	122	120	128	137			
5.25 lakhs	100	109	121	113	119	122	125	124	129	129	134	140			
7.5 lakhs	100	107	117	115	120	124	125	130	129	128	140	150			
9.75 lakhs	100	103	111	113	117	114	122	128	125	122	136	147			
12.5 lakhs	100	105	115	118	122	127	134	137	139	134	150	166	Medium PAT	185	6%
17.5 lakhs	100	107	114	120	126	130	139	144	141	140	158	174			
22.5 lakhs	100	108	115	124	125	133	141	148	149	144	163	179			
37.5 lakhs	100	103	111	119	124	131	145	151	151	148	171	190			
75 lakhs	100	105	113	122	132	142	157	169	166	162	193	215			
3 crores	100	102	109	126	136	149	172	188	189	199	250	284	High PAT	394	13%
7.5 crores	100	101	108	137	142	161	189	211	205	226	288	322			
17.5 crores	100	101	135	135	146	156	185	207	209	244	316	356			
37.5 crores	100	103	109	138	154	168	197	219	233	275	355	407			
75 crores	100	104	112	154	163	188	208	236	235	286	400	450			
300 crores	100	99	96	133	159	171	207	236	247	307	424	462			
More than 500 crores	100	103	85	137	144	161	183	215	203	282	406	478			

Figure 1: Profit After Tax (PAT) Progression Across PAT Categories

Source: Income Tax Department, Ministry of finance

Midpoint of PAT buckets	FY12	FY13	FY14	FY15	FY16	FY17	FY18	FY19	FY20	FY21	FY22	FY23	PAT category	10 yr avg share for each PAT group
75K	0.06%	0.06%	0.08%	0.05%	0.05%	0.04%	0.04%	0.03%	0.03%	0.03%	0.02%	0.02%		
1.75 lakhs	0.03%	0.03%	0.04%	0.02%	0.02%	0.02%	0.02%	0.01%	0.01%	0.01%	0.01%	0.01%		
2.25 lakhs	0.03%	0.03%	0.04%	0.02%	0.02%	0.02%	0.02%	0.01%	0.01%	0.01%	0.01%	0.01%		
3 lakhs	0.05%	0.06%	0.07%	0.04%	0.04%	0.04%	0.03%	0.03%	0.03%	0.02%	0.02%	0.02%		
3.75 lakhs	0.03%	0.03%	0.03%	0.02%	0.02%	0.02%	0.02%	0.02%	0.02%	0.01%	0.01%	0.01%	Low PAT	0.4%
4.25 lakhs	0.03%	0.03%	0.04%	0.02%	0.02%	0.02%	0.02%	0.02%	0.02%	0.01%	0.01%	0.01%		
4.75 lakhs	0.03%	0.03%	0.04%	0.02%	0.02%	0.02%	0.02%	0.02%	0.02%	0.01%	0.01%	0.01%		
5.25 lakhs	0.03%	0.03%	0.04%	0.02%	0.02%	0.02%	0.02%	0.02%	0.02%	0.01%	0.01%	0.01%		
7.5 lakhs	0.22%	0.23%	0.28%	0.18%	0.18%	0.17%	0.15%	0.13%	0.13%	0.10%	0.08%	0.07%		
9.75 lakhs	0.03%	0.03%	0.04%	0.02%	0.02%	0.02%	0.02%	0.02%	0.02%	0.01%	0.01%	0.01%		
12.5 lakhs	0.3%	0.3%	0.3%	0.2%	0.2%	0.2%	0.2%	0.2%	0.2%	0.1%	0.1%	0.1%		
17.5 lakhs	0.2%	0.2%	0.3%	0.2%	0.2%	0.2%	0.2%	0.2%	0.2%	0.1%	0.1%	0.1%		
22.5 lakhs	0.2%	0.2%	0.3%	0.2%	0.2%	0.2%	0.2%	0.2%	0.2%	0.1%	0.1%	0.1%		
37.5 lakhs	0.9%	1.0%	1.1%	0.8%	0.8%	0.8%	0.7%	0.7%	0.7%	0.5%	0.4%	0.4%		
75 lakhs	1.4%	1.5%	1.7%	1.3%	1.3%	1.2%	1.2%	1.1%	1.1%	0.8%	0.7%	0.7%	Medium PAT	2.5%
3 crores	4.9%	4.9%	5.7%	4.5%	4.5%	4.5%	4.5%	4.2%	4.4%	3.6%	3.2%	3.2%		
7.5 crores	3.1%	3.0%	3.6%	3.1%	3.0%	3.1%	3.1%	3.0%	3.0%	2.6%	2.3%	2.3%		
17.5 crores	5.3%	5.2%	5.9%	5.3%	5.3%	5.1%	5.3%	5.1%	5.3%	4.7%	4.4%	4.3%		
37.5 crores	4.8%	4.8%	5.6%	4.8%	5.0%	4.9%	5.0%	4.8%	5.3%	4.8%	4.4%	4.4%		
75 crores	5.3%	5.3%	6.4%	6.0%	5.9%	6.1%	5.9%	5.8%	5.9%	5.6%	5.6%	5.4%		
300 crores	16.0%	15.5%	16.4%	15.7%	17.3%	16.8%	17.7%	17.5%	18.8%	18.0%	17.8%	16.8%		
More than 500 crores	57.0%	57.4%	51.9%	57.4%	55.9%	56.5%	55.7%	56.9%	54.8%	58.9%	60.6%	62.0%	High PAT	97.2%
Total	100.0%	100.0%	100.0%	100.0%	100.0%	100.0%	100.0%	100.0%	100.0%	100.0%	100.0%	100.0%		
Medium	3.1%	3.2%	3.7%	2.7%	2.7%	2.6%	2.5%	2.3%	2.3%	1.7%	1.4%	1.4%		
High	96.4%	96.3%	95.6%	96.8%	96.9%	97.0%	97.2%	97.4%	97.4%	98.0%	98.4%	98.4%		

Figure 2: Profit After Tax Earned by Each of the PAT Categories (Expressed as a % of Total PAT)

Source: Income Tax Department, Ministry of finance

How to Read Figure 1

- 'Midpoint of PAT buckets' refers to the central point of each of the income buckets as reported by the Income Tax Department. For instance, the midpoint of Rs 75,000 refers to the PAT bucket of Rs 0 to Rs 1.5 lakh.

- The first column (FY12) is when the data series begins. Hence FY12 has been normalized to 100 for all the income buckets. Subsequently the entries represent just the growth over this normalized figure. The underlying data is the sum of gross total income (or PAT) for each PAT bucket as reported by the Income Tax Department. The underlying data as per the Income Tax Department was stated in Rs crore.

- Each of the income or PAT buckets was then classified under three super-segments, based on a simple classification criteria —PAT from Rs 0 to Rs 10 lakh is 'low PAT', from Rs 10 lakh to Rs 1 crore 'medium PAT', and Rs 1 crore onwards is 'high PAT'.

- The indexed numbers (starting from 100 in FY12) are then averaged across these three super segments for FY22. These are used to calculate the ten-year CAGR for each super segment, assuming the starting point is the same (100) for all.

How to Read Figure 2

- 'Midpoint of PAT buckets' is the same as for Figure 1.

- The columns for each year under the headings FY12, FY13 . . . to FY22 are simply the summation of gross total income (or PAT) in each bucket (as reported by the Income Tax Department) as a percentage of the total gross income for each year across buckets. For example, the cell showing Rs 75,000 under FY12 is just the summation of PAT in that bucket as a percentage of the total PAT in the FY12 column.

- Using the same labelling for PAT buckets as mentioned in the method for Figure 1, an average across the percentages for the last ten years was calculated, which is presented in the right-most column of the table. As the final column shows, the low, medium and high PAT buckets, accounts for 0.2 per cent, 2.5 per cent and 97 per cent of India's PAT respectively. Just as in high stakes sports tournaments like Wimbledon, so in India, a tiny minority of winners take home almost all the spoils in a free market economy. This is the 'Power Law' at work.

Further Reading

If you would like to delve deeper into the subjects which we have discussed in this book then you might want to turn to the following books.

- *India: A Million Mutinies Now* (1990) by V.S. Naipaul
  Although written in the late 1980s, the book's style and substance is such that it feels as if it was written a couple of years ago. Naipaul presciently captured how India is moving forward, not just economically but also socially. What lesser commentators saw as unrest and social turmoil was expertly reinterpreted by Naipaul as long suppressed voices challenging the Brahmin, Kshatriya and Bania hegemony. The author's acute ability to perceive social change is allied to his deep psychological insights into what makes Indians tick and why their ability to find their way in the world in the midst of enormous social churn gives the country dynamism and energy. A fitting climax to Naipaul's trilogy of books on India, the Nobel laureate sets a high bar for anyone else who aspires to write a non-fiction about India. If you have time to read only one book on India, this should be that book.

- *Desperately Seeking Shah Rukh: India's Lonely Young Women and the Search for Intimacy and Independence* (2022) by Shrayana Bhattacharya.

Ms Bhattacharya, a Harvard-trained economist working for the World Bank in South Asia, expertly uses Bollywood megastar Shah Rukh Khan's ascent as a narrative device to capture how Indian women, of all classes and ages, are relentless in their search for intimacy, independence and fun. The book is both a commentary on the oppressive masculinity prevalent in many parts of Indian society and a 'tapestry of encounters' showcasing how women navigate modern day India. Original, refreshing and in-your-face, Ms Bhattacharya's book is a lot of fun to read for both sexes (although the men might squirm in their seats a little bit).

- *Rebooting India: Realizing a Billion Aspirations* (2016) by Nandan Nilekani and Viral Shah
  Infosys co-founder Nandan Nilekani and Aadhaar designer Viral Shah explain the many use cases of Aadhaar and the monumental effect its usage would have for Indian public service. The authors lay out radical new ways of integrating tech and governance by restructuring the government-citizen relationship and eliminating age old methods of transaction and provision. Even as many of the use cases proposed by the authors have already come to pass in the years that have elapsed since the book was published, as a measure of the formidable tech talent at India's disposal as the country seeks to break out of grinding poverty, the book is a life-affirming read. Readers are introduced to a vastly different version of India, one that is far more optimised and equitable than the India we live in today.

- *Ants among Elephants: An Untouchable Family and the Making of Modern India* (2017) by Sujatha Gidla
  This autobiography is an emotional—sometimes stomach churningly so—account of the hardships

that Ms Gidla's family endured in post-Independent India, on account of being deemed to be part of the untouchable community in Andhra Pradesh. Written through testimonies and anecdotes of her mother, uncles and friends, Ms Gidla—a conductor on the New York City subway and a self-declared Communist—showcases the raw deal that India gives to its oppressed castes. Ms Gidla's descriptions of her mother's personal struggles as an untouchable woman and the graphic descriptions of murder and bloodshed in modern day southern India make the book an essential read for those who still harbour romantic notions about India being a land populated by gentle, non-violent people.

- *Makers of Modern India* (2012) by Ramachandra Guha
Mr Guha chronicles the written works of nineteen influential political figures from the nineteenth and early twentieth century India. A collection of the writings of India's greatest ever thinkers and activists, the book contains useful summaries of the work of icons such as Mahatma Gandhi and Babasaheb Ambedkar whilst also highlighting the contributions of lesser-known figures such as Hamid Dalwai and Tarabai Shinde. It touches on topics of class, nationalism, the future of a free India and equal rights for women. Ram Guha's literary portraits of India's greatest thinkers is a captivating read because it brings out the depth of thought and prescience of the thinkers who guided India not just to Independence but also well beyond that.

- *The Economic History of India, 1857 to 2010* (2020) by Tirthankar Roy
A compilation of India's economic journey from colonial rule to the present day, Tirthankar Roy, a Professor at the London School of Economics, blends economic

data analysis with extensive literature surveys (of the works of other historians and economists). By diving deep into industry, employment, shifts in agriculture, finance and urban life, this book offers a comprehensive guide to understanding how India became the fifth largest economy in the world and yet remained one of the poorest fifty countries in the world as measured by per capita income.

- *Half a Billion Rising: The Emergence of Indian Women* (2015) by Anirudha Dutta
  Written a decade ago by our friend Anirudha Dutta, *Half a Billion Rising* presciently predicted the rapid social and economic ascent of Indian women. Anirudha's book chronicles the shifts in gender norms and the gender equality landscape across small-town India through the voices of these very women. First, he explores the lives of Indian women in previous generations, who were oppressed and socio-economically challenged and stopped from spreading their wings. Identifying education as the primary driver of change for young girls in modern India, Anirudha then takes a look at how these changes are being reflected in modern media such as television and advertisements.

- *Sisterhood Economy: Of, By, For Women* (2022) by Shaili Chopra
  Former television journalist Shaili Chopra emphasizes the importance of Indian women not only to India itself but to the world as a whole. Readers are offered a comprehensive analysis of the systematic faults and barriers hindering women from rising and how technology, agency and 'sisterhood' are changing that. Highlighting the lack of exposure and inclusion given to women in India, Chopra

brings to light the lesser-known stories of Indian women with a powerful message for equality.

- *South vs North: India's Great Divide* (2023) by R.S. Nilakantan
  Modern day India shows a sharp contrast in quality of life across the nation. On an average, a child growing up in South India today will have a higher chance of attaining education, reliable healthcare, gainful employment and a long life. Yet the unfreezing of Lok Sabha seat allotments in 2026 will punish South Indian states for their effective policies, granting them fewer seats due to these states being less populated than their North Indian counterparts. Nilakantan explores the reasons for this disparity in development between North and South India, tracing the different paths Indian states have taken since 1947. Identifying key flaws in the Indian Union as we know it, he proposes a new model, one that is not dissimilar to the Athenian model so that India can become a nation of parity once more.

- *India's New Capitalists* (2008) by Harish Damodaran
  Acclaimed author and journalist Harish Damodaran takes a deep dive into how capitalism has evolved in liberalised India, 'spanning a whole range of industries' and become increasingly more inclusive, covering a greater variety of social classes and strata. He does so by examining a varied number of communities and sectors, such as the sugar industry in the South and farming communities in the North. Additionally, he examines the specifics of particular groups such as the Marathas and Patidars, detailing the influence that politics and other factors have had on capitalist trends in India in the past and today.

- *Dreamers: How Young Indians Are Changing the World* (2018) by Snigdha Poonam
  From aspiring politicians to budding entrepreneurs, the India of tomorrow is being shaped by its youth today whom author Snigdha Poonam terms 'The Angry Young Men (and Women).' The book looks at the life of university students in India's Tier 2 cities such as Allahabad and Ranchi amid political protests and rallies. With her keen eye for behavioural and situational detail, Ms Poonam—who now lives in London—paints a vivid picture of the evolving socio-cultural dynamics in India through intimate stories and first-hand accounts of the lives of the Indian youth, fighting stereotypes and traditional norms and often doing so without realising how powerful their small acts of freedom can be.

- *Another Sort of Freedom* (2023) by Gurcharan Das
  Gurcharan Das' multiple bestselling books have shown our generation how one can evaluate through one's personal viewpoint and then skillfully extrapolate that to draw more general lessons about the country at large. In his autobiography, Mr. Das gives another masterclass on how to deploy this skill to create an arresting narrative. 'The India Unbound' author explains his lifelong search for 'lightness' or 'something more than just Moksha'. His father, spiritual yet a man of science, had a profound effect on him from early on, and his words of 'making a life' rather than 'making a living' still reverberate with Mr. Das. At a personal level, this guiding principle helped Mr. Das make pivotal yet difficult choices—right from taking up philosophy at Harvard rather than a functional course like engineering to leaving the humdrum of a thriving corporate career to become a full-time writer—quite

effortlessly, eventually developing the mantra of taking only one's work seriously and not oneself.

- *Power and Progress: Our Thousand Year Struggle Over Technology and Prosperity* (2023) by Simon Johnson and Daron Acemoglu
Going against the tide of the popular narrative—which says that technological progress brings widespread prosperity—the authors suggest that we revisit our understanding of the concepts of 'progress' and 'prosperity'. The authors use several examples to demonstrate how the interplay between technological advancement and economic gains for society as a whole is not as straightforward as it seems. More specifically, the authors say that contemporary technological 'progress' is again enriching a small group of entrepreneurs and investors whilst driving up the cost of living for much of the rest of society. Naturally, therefore, the authors suggest a range of policy measures to keep inequality in check. Whilst the book is written in the Western context, given that India's services economy (which accounts for the majority of its GDP) is highly integrated with the global economy, the book has immense relevance for decision makers in India.

- *The End of the World is Just the Beginning: Mapping the Collapse of Globalization* (2022) by Peter Zeihan
Several years ago, American geopolitical expert Peter Zeihan, presciently predicted China's collapse—economically and politically. Few believed him then and now as they eat humble pie with Mr. Zeihan's *New York Times* bestseller for company, he finds himself in high demand not just in the conference circuit but also in the boardrooms of multinational companies. Whilst the book is relatively bullish about America (as per Mr Zeihan it is the best placed amongst the world's

leading economies), it also surprisingly constructive about India. This book, therefore, has therapeutic value for readers accustomed to reading relentlessly upbeat accounts of China's Communist controlled economy alongside faint praise for poor, democratic India.

- *The Billionaire Raj: A Journey Through India's New Gilded Age* (2018) by James Crabtree
  Whilst James Crabtree's in-depth exploration of the underbelly of Indian capitalism is unlikely to have endeared him to the Indian elite, the book is a great introduction to those who want to understand how business and politics interplay in India, especially in sectors with heavy state interference. Divided into three separate parts, the book gives the reader a clear view of the roots of corruption in India, the rise of certain high-profile capitalists who rub shoulders with politicians on a daily basis and the ushering in of a *New Gilded Age* in the world's largest democracy. If the 2020s are India's equivalent of the 'Jazz Age' then the protagonists of Mr. Crabtree's book will go down in posterity much as Carnegie, JP Morgan and Vanderbilt did.

Notes

Preface

1 Joshua Felman and Daniel Leigh, published in April 2011 (attached pdf) https://www.imf.org/-/media/ Websites/IMF/imported-flagship-issues/external/pubs/ft/ weo/2011/01/c1/_box14pdf.ashx)
2 Power Laws in Economics: An Introduction; author - Xavier Gabaix (apa citation - Gabaix, X. (2016). Power laws in economics: An introduction. Journal of Economic Perspectives, 30(1), 185–206.) https://www.aeaweb.org/ articles?id=10.1257/jep.30.1.185
3 Wimbledon website - (attached pdf) https://www. wimbledon.com/pdf/The_Championships_2023_ Prize%20Money.pdf

Prologue

1 Images sourced from the internet (left one from Reddit and right one from *Deccan Herald*); images used only for illustration purposes, their copyrights remain with their respective creators)
2 https://www.indiatoday.in/magazine/economy/story/ 19970804-real-estate-business-in-india-faces-unprece dented-crisis-as-prices-plummets-831849-1997–08–03

3 Image on the left from Google Maps, and the one of the right from Bing images. The images here are only for illustration purposes, their copyrights remain with their respective creators)

4 Bing images; images used only for illustration purposes, their copyrights remain with their respective creators

5 https://www.bing.com/search?q=electronic+city+bangalore+employees&qs=n&form=QBRE&sp=-1&lq=0&pq=electronic+city+bangalore+employee&sc=6-34&sk=&cvid=E7A500B4015045DFB3F-AD395E9E6E709&ghsh=0&ghacc=0&ghpl=

6 Images sourced from Marcellus Investment Managers

7 https://www.electronic-city.in/companies/

8 https://des.karnataka.gov.in/storage/pdf-files/Economic%20Survey%202022–23%20English.pdf

9 https://data.opencity.in/dataset/economic-survey-of-maharashtra-2022–23

10 https://www.electronic-city.in/about/geography

11 Data on property rental costs in Electronic City sourced from 99acres: https://www.99acres.com/commercial-land-for-rent-in-electronic-city-bangalore-south-ffid

12 PM recently said govt doing everything to double farmers' income; author: Anju Agnihotri Chaba; Date of publication: March 3 2021; updated link: https://indianexpress.com/article/cities/chandigarh/pm-said-govt-doing-everything-double-farmers-income-7212127/sourced from the Indian Express

13 Average salary in Hosur in Manufacturing from Payscale. com; updated link: https://www.payscale.com/research/IN/Location=Hosur-Tamil-Nadu/Salary

14 No. of factory employees in South India from Annual Survey of Industries (2019–20); sourced from National Data Archive of MOSPI: https://microdata.gov.in/nada43/index.php/catalog/158

15 https://www.nabard.org/demo/auth/writereaddata/
    tender/2110164635BENGALURU%20URBAN%20
    PLP%202016–17%20FINAL.3–9.pdf
16 https://www.financialexpress.com/business/sme-msme-
    fin-number-of-msmes-shut-in-fy23-so-far-doubles-from-
    fy22-heres-why-3008692/

Chapter 1: How India Changed Its Master Narrative

1   https://en.wikipedia.org/wiki/Gukesh_D
2   https://www.nytimes.com/2024/04/24/crosswords/chess/
    gukesh-candidates-winner.html#:~:text=Dommaraju%20
    Gukesh%2C%20a%2017%2Dyear%2Dold%20Indian%20
    grandmaster%2C,qualify%20for%20the%20title%20match.
3   https://indianexpress.com/article/sports/chess/
    gukesh-interview-candidates-2024-victory-toronto-
    9287058/#:~:text=%E2%80%9CI%20came%20to%20
    Toronto%20with,I%20would%20have%20every%20chance.
4   https://khelnow.com/chess/2023–12-chess-grandmasters-
    india
5   https://en.wikipedia.org/wiki/List_of_Indian_chess_
    players
6   https://khelnow.com/chess/2023–12-female-chess-
    grandmasters-india
7   https://indianexpress.com/article/sports/chess/
    viswanathan-anand-on-indian-players-world-title-
    express-adda-9459681/
8   https://www.hindustantimes.com/sports/others/jyothi-
    yarraji-confident-of-running-faster-now-says-coach-
    james-hillier-101720284758610.html
9   https://www.researchgate.net/publication/305201517_
    Personal_Master_and_Alternative_Narratives_An_
    Integrative_Framework_for_Understanding_Identity_
    Development_in_Context

10 https://nationalinterest.org/blog/buzz/how-china-defeated-india-terrifying-1962-war-122406

11 https://ourworldindata.org/famines#all-charts

12 https://econ.st/3xjIHj8

13 https://pib.gov.in/PressReleaseIframePage.aspx?PRID=1980171

14 https://economictimes.indiatimes.com/news/india/uttarkashi-tunnel-how-jhansi-rat-miners-rescued-workers-after-high-tech-american-machine-failed/articleshow/105558802.cms?from=mdr

15 South Asia Terrorism Portal; data recorded up to 18 December 2023; *Data since 6 March 2000; for data from 1994 to1999, data does not include fatalities from left-wing extremism; data compiled from news reports, and is provisional

16 Over 167,000 businesses set up in FY22, the highest in 3 years; author: Gulveen Aulakh; date of publication: Apr 19 2022; source: The Livemint. https://www.livemint.com/news/india/india-creates-1–7-lakh-new-companies-in-fy22-growth-in-new-registration-slows-11650276610417.html#:~:text=As%20many%20as%20167%2C076%20companies,were%20set%20up%20in%20FY20.

17 Number of companies registered year wise sourced from Ministry of Corporate Affairs; updated link: https://www.mca.gov.in/content/mca/global/en/data-and-reports/company-statistics/indian-foreign-companies-llps/total-companies-registered/archive.html

18 Basole, A., Abraham, R., Rakshit, A., Vijayamba, R., Shrivastava, A., & Halder, T. (2023). State of working India 2023: Social identities and labour market outcomes.

19 Deshpande, A., & Ramachandran, R. (2019). Traditional hierarchies and affirmative action in a globalizing economy: Evidence from India. World Development, 118, 63–78.

20 Report of the Household Finance Committee, 2017

21 This is a database for UPI (statistics) and not a publication. https://www.npci.org.in/what-we-do/upi/product-statistics

22 This is a quote by Vladimir Ilyich Lenin. https://www.
goodreads.com/quotes/342783-there-are-decades-where-
nothing-happens-and-there-are-weeks

Chapter 2: A Century Spent Answering Four Questions

1 Bing images; images used only for illustration purposes,
their copyrights remain with their respective creators
2 Forget Teslas, India's EV revolution is happening
on two wheels; publication - The Economist; date of
Publication - Apr 20 2023. https://www.economist.com/
asia/2023/04/20/forget-teslas-indias-ev-revolution-is-
happening-on-two-wheels
3 B.R. Tomlinson, in *A History of Economic Thoughts in India*
by Ajit Dasgupta (2002)
4 Also see Jacob Viner's *Studies in the Theory of International
Trade*, [1937])
5 Bankim Chandra Chatterjee quoted in *A History of Economic
Thought in India* by Ajit Dasgupta (2002)
6 From *A History of Economic Thought in India* by Ajit
Dasgupta (2002)
7 As quoted in *A History of Economic Thought in India*, by Ajit
Dasgupta (2002)
8 Source: Britannica Money; author: Karl Montevirgen;
link: https://www.britannica.com/money/comparative-
advantage. http://bit.ly/49r5Oup
9 From *The Economy of Modern India: From 1860 to the
Twenty First Century* (2013)

Chapter 3: How Policymakers Have Driven Economic Change in India

1 World Bank
2 Our World in Data Famine Dataset (sourced from multiple
publications); authors in OWID - Joe Hasell and Max

Roser (first published in 2013 and last revised in 2024 april) https://ourworldindata.org/famines#all-charts

3   D. Rodrik & A. Subramanian, 'From "Hindu Growth" to productivity surge: the mystery of the Indian growth transition', *IMF Staff Papers*, 2005, *52*(2), pp. 193–228.

4   RBI report on Current Account Dynamics (part 1 or 2) - 2004. https://www.rbi.org.in/scripts/PublicationReportDetails. aspx?ID=357

5   Length of National Highway in India from FY03 to FY23 in km; published by Shangliao Sun; sourced from Statista; updated link - https://www.statista.com/statistics/729992/ india-length-of-national-highways/

6   Air passengers carried in India from World Bank (International Civil Aviation organization, Civil Aviation Statistics of the world and ICAO staff estimates); updated link - https://data. worldbank.org/indicator/IS.AIR.PSGR?locations=IN

7   Number of households with access to internet in mn from Statista; published by J. Degenhard in Jul 2024; updated link - https://www.statista.com/forecasts/1143584/internet-households-in-india

8   RBI Report of committee on financial inclusion (date - 2015). https://linkedin.us19.list-manage.com/track/click?u=52ada 2ee20240692fbeb44407&id=5497d8d6a1&e=9174 5b5270

9   'RBI Annual Report 2022–23: Less than 50% of deposits with banks are insured; here's what it means' by Teena Jain Kaushal on May 30 2023 for Business Today (Money Today); updated link - https://www.businesstoday.in/personal-finance/ insurance/story/rbi-annual-report-2022–23-less-than-50-of-deposits-with-banks-are-insured-heres-what-it-means-383439–2023–05–30#:~:text=According%20to%20the%20la-test%20RBI,of%20accounts%20(300.1%20crore).

10 'UPI transactions itness slight fall, clocks 9.3 bn in June '23' by Anushka Sengupta for ET BFSI on Jul 3 2023;

updated link: https://bfsi.economictimes.indiatimes.com/
news/fintech/upi-transactions-witness-slight-fall-clocks-
9–3-bln-in-june23/101455226#:~:text=Unified%20
Payments%20Interface%20%28UPI%29%20recorded%20
a%20slight%20downfall,according%20to%20National%20
Payments%20Corporation%20of%20India%E2%80
%99s%20%28NPCI%29.

11 https://data.worldbank.org/indicator/SE.XPD.TOTL.
GD.ZS?locations=IN

12 https://www.bing.com/search?q=indian+government+heal
thcare+spend+as+a+%25+of+GDP+in+2015&qs=n&form
=QBRE&sp=-1&lq=0&pq=indian+government+healthcar
e+spend+as+a+%25+of+gdp+in+201&sc=0–55&sk=&cvid
=25279BB254374AD897166A93F56C7520&ghsh=0&gh
acc=0&ghpl=

13 https://static.pib.gov.in/WriteReadData/specificdocs/
documents/2022/feb/doc20222814101.pdf

14 https://www.moneycontrol.com/news/business/budget/
economic-survey-2023-govt-spent-2–1-of-gdp-on-
healthcare-in-fy23–9970751.html#:~:text=The%20
Economic%20Survey%202023%20tabled%20in%20
the%20Rajya,before%20was%202.2%20per%20cent%20
of%20the%20GDP.

15 https://linkedin.us19.list-manage.com/track/
click?u=52ada2ee20240692fbeb44407&id=711fe08dc0&e
=91745b5270

16 https://linkedin.us19.list-manage.com/track/
click?u=52ada2ee20240692fbeb44407&id=3d1307394a&e
=91745b5270

17 https://linkedin.us19.list-manage.com/track/
click?u=52ada2ee20240692fbeb44407&id=8f47778efd&e
=91745b5270

18 https://www.telegraphindia.com/india/five-assembly-
polls-to-have-8–2-crore-male-7–8-crore-female-voters-
election-commission/cid/1972152

19 https://www.livemint.com/news/india/ladli-behna-scheme-mp-govt-hikes-financial-aid-35-reservation-in-govt-jobs-for-women-ahead-of-rakhi-11693153609198.html

20 https://dbtbharat.gov.in/

21 https://www.npci.org.in/PDF/nach/dbt/DBT_User_Codes_as_of_15062023.pdf

22 https://www.bqprime.com/opinion/the-politics-of-economics-signals-from-the-election-campaign

23 https://cepr.org/voxeu/columns/internationalising-chinas-equity-markets-role-domestic-and-foreign-investors

24 https://www.cdslindia.com/Publications/FIIFPIInvstmntFinYrData.aspx

25 https://www.ceicdata.com/en/indicator/china/foreign-portfolio-investment

26 https://www.ceicdata.com/en/indicator/india/foreign-portfolio-investment

27 https://www.business-standard.com/finance/news/household-savings-rate-plummeted-to-five-decade-low-in-2022–23-rbi-123100600852_1.html

28 https://www.thehindu.com/business/pharma-exports-grew-a-shade-better-to-2539-bn-in-fy23/article66737982.ece#:~:text=India%E2%80%99s%20pharmaceutical%20exports%20totalled%20%2425.39%20billion%20in%20FY23%2C,the%20Russia-Ukraine%20war%2C%20hampered%20the%20pace%20of%20growth.

29 https://investopedia365.com/remittances-to-india-grew-26-to-112–5-billion-in-fy23/#:~:text=Remittances%20to%20the%20country%20by%20non-resident%20Indians%20rose,Remittances%20to%20India%20were%20%2489.1%20billion%20in%20FY22.

30 https://marcellus.in/blogs/midnight-approaches-for-indias-retail-lending-boom/

Chapter 4: The Rise of Indian Women

1 https://www.indiatoday.in/india/story/pm-awas-gramin-yojana-married-women-flee-lovers-uttar-pradesh-money-2564120-2024-07-09

2 https://economictimes.indiatimes.com/small-biz/entrepreneurship/the-rise-of-women-in-entrepreneurial-roles-in-india/articleshow/108317138.cms?from=mdr

3 https://www.census2011.co.in/census/district/304-dewas.html

4 https://medium.com/meesho-tech/inspired-by-the-women-of-his-hometown-pavan-patil-is-helping-meesho-entrepreneurs-succeed-46f776cd5ae0

5 https://www.linkedin.com/pulse/half-billion-rising-what-i-learnt-surprised-me-anirudha-dutta/

6 https://www.education.gov.in/sites/upload_files/mhrd/files/statistics-new/ESAG-2018.pdf

7 https://www.livemint.com/education/news/cbse-class-12-result-2023-girls-outshine-boys-by-6-per-cent-in-terms-of-pass-percentage-11683871070235.html#:~:text=The%20Central%20Board%20of%20Secondary,stood%20at%2087.33%20per%20cent.

8 Future of Global Wealth Management report by BCG and Kotak Wealth Management, 2020

9 https://web-assets.bcg.com/img-src/BCG-Why-Women-Owned-Startups-Are-a-Better-Bet-May-2018-NL_tcm9-193585.pdf

10 https://mospi.gov.in/sites/default/files/publication_reports/women-men22/WomenMen2022.pdf

11 https://marcellus.in/blogs/exit-traditional-capitalism-enter-capitalism-without-capital/

12 https://www.ilo.org/newdelhi/info/public/fs/WCMS_857392/lang-en/index.htm

13 https://www.mospi.gov.in/sites/default/files/publication_
   reports/AnnualReportPLFS2021–22F1.pdf
14 https://www.thehindu.com/news/national/women-in-
   tech-earn-7-more-than-men-on-average-but-men-snag-
   highest-salaries/article66591413.ece
15 https://tech.hindustantimes.com/tech/news/
   how-many-aadhaar-numbers-in-india-find-out-
   here-71633178675185.html#:~:text=It%20has%20
   been%20revealed%20that%2C%20as%20on%20
   date%2C,166%20more%20standalone%20Aadhaar%20
   enrolment%20and%20update%20centres.
16 https://www.businesstoday.in/personal-finance/
   insurance/story/rbi-annual-report-2022–23-less-than-
   50-of-deposits-with-banks-are-insured-heres-what-
   it-means-383439–2023–05–30#:~:text=According%20
   to%20the%20latest%20RBI,of%20accounts%20
   (300.1%20crore).
17 https://www.rbi.org.in/scripts/publicationreportdetails.
   aspx?id=836#CH1
18 https://www.statista.com/statistics/1388218/india-
   online-bpc-market-revenue-share-by-company/
19 H.R. Diner, *The Jews of the United States, 1654 to 2000*
   (Vol. 4), University of California Press, 2004.
20 S. Ravi (n.d.). 'Women and Electoral Politics: The Good,
   Bad and Ugly'. (Retrieved July 19, 2024, from https://
   www.brookings.edu/wp-content/uploads/2017/03/
   missing-women-in-indian-democracy.pdf)
21 Census 2011 database for Chhattisgarh. https://www.
   census2011.co.in/data/town/802062-kondagaon-
   chhattisgarh.html
22 Goldin, C. (2006). The quiet revolution that transformed
   women's employment, education, and family. American
   economic review, 96(2), 1–21. https://scholar.harvard.
   edu/files/goldin/files/the_quiet_revolution_that_

transformed_womens_employment_education_and_
family.pdf

23 Implementation of household electrification under
Saubhagya and RDSS - GOI Press Release on 23 Dec 2023;
updated link: https://pib.gov.in/PressReleaseIframePage.
aspx?PRID=1989801

24 https://ppac.gov.in/uploads/rep_studies/1708084478_
LPG_Profile_Report_1_1_2024%20_Web.
pdf#:~:text=As%20on%201.1.2024%20PSU%20
OMCs%20%28IOCL%2C%20BPCL%20and,who%20
are%20being%20served%20by%2025%2C449%20
LPG%20distributors.

25 Jal Jeevan Mission Dashboard, Government of India.
https://ejalshakti.gov.in/jjmreport/JJMIndia.aspx

Chapter 5: The Rise of a New, Educated Elite

1 India Internet penetration rate from Statista (published in
May 2024 by Tanushree Basuroy). https://www.statista.
com/statistics/792074/india-internet-penetration-rate/

2 College pedigree, daddy's name, BBC accent no longer
golden ticket. India has a growing new elite - by Shekhar
Gupta for The Print in June 2023. https://theprint.in/
national-interest/college-pedigree-daddys-name-bbc-
accent-no-longer-golden-ticket-india-has-a-growing-
new-elite/1621127/

3 Forget IIT, IIM degrees. The inspiring story of CRED
founder Kunal Shah who once worked as a data entry
operator - by ET Online in Feb 2024 for Economic
Times Panache. https://economictimes.indiatimes.com/
magazines/panache/forget-iit-iim-degrees-the-inspiring-
story-of-cred-founder-kunal-shah-who-once-worked-
as-a-data-entry-operator/articleshow/107475170.
cms?utm_source=contentofinterest&utm_
medium=text&utm_campaign=cppst

4   'In the last three years, India has added almost 58,000 crorepati taxpayers—a jump of 51%. What has scripted this unusual trend?' - The Economic Times (19th August 2023) by Shantanu Nandan Sharma.

5   India Private Equity Report 2023.Trial by fire: Indian PE ecosystem stays resilient in a globally challenging year. By Arpan Sheth, Sriwatsan Krishnan, Aditya Shukla, Prabhav Kashyap, and Ronika Sapra April 19, 2023 (updated link-https://www.bain.com/insights/india-private-equity-report-2023/)

6   IIFL Capital's own research - I can share the underlying file IIFL Research.

7   RSPL group website information, https://www.rsplgroup.com/aboutus

8   Audit Bureau of Circulations: Highest circulated dailies weeklies and magazines amongst member publications (across languages) as on 11th April 2023. http://www.auditbureau.org/files/JD%202022%20Highest%20Circulated%20(across%20languages).pdf

9   DB Corp's website information. https://dbcorpltd.com/index.php

10   DB Corp information on Value research. https://www.valueresearchonline.com/stocks/45319/db-corp-ltd/

Chapter 6: The Explosive Ascent of Peninsular India

1   https://www.pib.gov.in/PressReleasePage.aspx?PRID=1942055

2   https://indianexpress.com/article/explained/explained-economics/explained-tamil-nadus-decentralised-industrialisation-model-9272702/

3   Sources: National Crime Record Bureau, Ministry of Home Affairs (2021) and https://en.wikipedia.org/wiki/List_of_countries_by_intentional_homicide_rate

4   https://www.thehindu.com/news/national/
     understanding-the-delimitation-exercise-explained/
     article67819203.ece
5   Ministry of External Affairs (link - https://www.mea.gov.
     in/Uploads/PublicationDocs/19167_State_wise_seats_
     in_Lok_Sabha_18–03–2009.pdf)

Chapter 7: China's Unravelling Creates a $300-billion+ Opportunity

1   Zachary Karabell, Superfusion – *How China and America
     Became One Economy and Why the World's Prosperity
     Depends on It* (2009)
2   *China's Rise – Challenges and Opportunities*, by C. Fred
     Bergstein, Charles Freeman, Nicholas R. Lardy, and
     Derek J. Mitchel (2008)
3   China's relationship with the U.S. By Christine Huang,
     Laura Silver, and Laura Clancy on May 1 2024. https://
     www.pewresearch.org/global/2024/05/01/chinas-
     relationship-with-the-u-s/
4   Chinese spy balloon gathered intelligence from sensitive
     U.S. military sites, despite U.S. efforts to block it - by
     Courtney Kube and Carol E. Lee for NBC News on April
     3   2023.   https://www.nbcnews.com/politics/national-
     security/china-spy-balloon-collected-intelligence-us-
     military-bases-rcna77155
5   Xi Jinping chooses 'yes' men over economic growth in
     politburo purge - By Helen Davidson and Verna Yu for
     the Guardian on 23 Oct 2022. https://www.theguardian.
     com/world/2022/oct/23/xi-jinping-chooses-yes-men-
     over-economic-growth-politburo-purge-china
6   India's direct tax collection jumps 20% to ₹18.9
     trillion - by Gireesh Chandra Prasad for the Mint
     on 19 March 2024. https://www.livemint.com/news/

indias-direct-tax-collections-jumps-20-to-rs-18–9-trillion-11710861926008.html

7   https://timesofindia.indiatimes.com/business/india-business/credit-growth-outstrips-deposit-increase-in-fy24/articleshow/109444453.cms

8   https://www.thehindubusinessline.com/economy/indian-automobile-industry-records-125-growth-in-fy24/article68057552.ece#:~:text=The%20Indian%20automobile%20industry%20posted,(SIAM)%20said%20on%20Friday.

9   https://virtuemarketresearch.com/report/smartphone-market

10   https://www.indiaherald.com/Technology/Read/994523142/Top-mobile-manufacturing-countries-in-the-world

11   https://www.livemint.com/economy/smartphones-fourth-largest-export-item-from-india-up-42-percent-to-15–6-billion-in-fy24-apple-samsung-wistron-pegatron-11716436491522.html

12   https://www.custommarketinsights.com/report/india-smartphone-market/

13   https://gtri.co.in/gtriRep9.pdf

14   https://www.financialexpress.com/industry/production-linked-incentive-scheme-reset-govt-may-shift-smartphone-pli-by-a-year/2266267/

15   https://www.cnbc.com/2024/04/10/apple-made-14-billion-worth-of-iphones-in-india-in-shift-from-china.html

16   https://www.statista.com/statistics/216459/global-market-share-of-apple-iphone/

17   https://www.business-standard.com/article/technology/every-fourth-iphone-will-be-made-in-india-by-2025-says-jp-morgan-analyst-122112101115_1.html

18   https://economictimes.indiatimes.com/industry/cons-products/electronics/dixon-technologies-china-plus-one-pli-scheme-throw-up-a-rising-star-that-shows-india-the-way/articleshow/109200705.cms?from=mdr

19   https://www.business-standard.com/industry/news/foxconn-apple-samsung-to-receive-rs-4–400-cr-under-smartphone-pli-scheme-124030400126_1.html

20   https://economictimes.indiatimes.com/industry/cons-products/electronics/electronics-companies-seek-rs-35000-crore-incentive-plan-for-components/articleshow/110444865.cms?from=mdr

21   https://www.grandviewresearch.com/industry-analysis/active-pharmaceutical-ingredients-market

22   https://daxueconsulting.com/api-industry-in-china/

23   https://www.grandviewresearch.com/industry-analysis/india-active-pharmaceutical-ingredients-market-report

24   https://www.praxisga.com/insights/pharma-and-life-sciences/india-s-road-to-freedom-from-chinese-api-dependence

25   https://www.business-standard.com/article/economy-policy/local-manufacturing-of-35-apis-started-after-pli-scheme-mansukh-mandaviya-122032901025_1.html

26   https://www.livemint.com/economy/pli-scheme-helps-start-production-of-22-key-bulk-drugs-11677001530692.html

27   https://www.fortuneindia.com/long-reads/the-api-man-of-laurus/109965

28   https://www.mordorintelligence.com/industry-reports/global-medical-device-technologies-market-industry

29   https://www.expertmarketresearch.com/reports/medical-devices-market

30   https://www.fortunebusinessinsights.com/press-release/medical-devices-market-9074

31 https://www.frontiersin.org/journals/public-health/
    articles/10.3389/fpubh.2022.875104/full
32 https://www.techsciresearch.com/report/india-medical-
    devices-market/8161.html
33 https://www.researchandmarkets.com/reports/5774591/
    medical-devices-market-in-india
34 https://www.investindia.gov.in/sector/medical-devices
35 https://www.usitc.gov/publications/332/journals/china_
    medtech_jice_508_compliant.pdf
36 https://www.investindia.gov.in/sector/medical-devices
37 https://pharmaceuticals.gov.in/sites/default/files/
    List%20of%20approved%20applicants%20under%20
    PLI%20Medical%20Devices-%20Dated%2006th%20
    November%2C%202023.pdf
38 https://www.ibef.org/industry/medical-
    devices#:~:text=As%20of%20May%202021%2C%20
    the,20%20medical%20devices%20markets%20globally
39 https://www.ibef.org/industry/medical-
    devices#:~:text=As%20of%20May%202021%2C%20
    the,20%20medical%20devices%20markets%20globally
40 https://www.keka.com/library/minimum-wages/
    maharashtra
41 https://www.timechamp.io/blogs/average-
    salary-in-bangladesh/#:~:text=Minimum%20
    Wage,63%2C480BDT%20(578.46%20USD).
42 https://sbi.co.in/web/interest-rates/interest-rates/
    benchmark-prime-lending-rate-historical-data
43 https://ycharts.com/indicators/china_loan_prime_
    rate#:~:text=China%20Loan%20Prime%20Rate%20
    (I%3ACLPR)&text=China%20Loan%20Prime%20
    Rate%20is,long%20term%20average%20of%203.76%25e
44 https://www.business-standard.com/finance/news/govt-
    plans-to-borrow-rs-7-5-trillion-from-market-in-first-
    half-of-fy25-124032700791_1.html

45 https://agupubs.onlinelibrary.wiley.com/doi/full/10.1029/2018GL081477#:~:text=During%20the%20era%20of%20British,people%20(Maharatna%2C%201996).

46 https://economictimes.indiatimes.com/news/economy/foreign-trade/indias-services-exports-grow-11–4-in-2023-unctad-report/articleshow/109602819.cms?from=mdr

47 https://takshashila.org.in/blogs/pli-schemes-in-india-whats-the-verdict

48 https://www.business-standard.com/opinion/columns/mobile-phone-pli-is-an-india-success-story-12306 1900903_1.html

49 https://www.nextias.com/blog/production-linked-incentive-pli/#:~:text=It%20aims%20to%20attract%20foreign,anchor%20investors%20managing%20new%20projects

Chapter 8: Outsourcing 2.0: The Global Capability Centre Boom

1 https://www.livemint.com/technology/ibm-goes-beyond-metros-for-talent-pool-cost-benefit-11650222934738.html

2 https://www.business-standard.com/industry/news/india-commands-over-50-of-global-capability-centres-retains-top-spot-124041200842_1.html

3 https://www.macrotrends.net/global-metrics/countries/USA/united-states/fertility-rate

4 https://www.ela.europa.eu/sites/default/files/2023–09/ELA-eures-shortages-surpluses-report-2022.pdf

5 https://www.uschamber.com/assets/documents/Pandemic-Unemployed-Survey-May-2022.pdf

6 https://www.uschamber.com/workforce/understanding-americas-labor-shortage

7   https://economictimes.indiatimes.com/topic/bpm
8   https://www.business-standard.com/industry/news/gccs-in-india-becoming-nerve-centres-for-global-business-success-124053001374_1.html
9   https://www.hindustantimes.com/education/news/aishe-report-24–16-lakh-students-graduate-from-ba-courses-highest-in-ug-level-101706360164634.html#:~:text=.(HT%20Photo)-,According%20to%20the%20report%2C%20the%20total%20number%20of%20pass%2Douts,discipline%20with%2011.97%20lakh%20graduates.
10   https://economictimes.indiatimes.com/tech/technology/global-companies-flock-to-indias-tier-ii-cities-for-new-capability-centers/articleshow/105791067.cms?from=mdr
11   https://economictimes.indiatimes.com/tech/technology/global-companies-flock-to-indias-tier-ii-cities-for-new-capability-centers/articleshow/105791067.cms?from=mdr
12   https://corporate.cyrilamarchandblogs.com/2024/05/optimal-locations-for-global-capability-centres-gccs-in-india-where-to-set-it-up/

Chapter 9: Creative Destruction on an Epic Scale

1   https://www.britannica.com/topic/churning-of-the-ocean-of-milk
2   'Capitalism, Socialism and Democracy' (1942) by Joseph Schumpeter
3   This is a database on IT department's website, https://incometaxindia.gov.in/Pages/Direct-Taxes-Data.aspx
4   Number of registered closed companies across India as of January 2024, by status - By Manya Rathore for Statista in Feb 2024 (survey time period until Jan 2024). https://www.statista.com/statistics/1008345/india-number-of-registered-closed-companies-by-status/

5   The Underdog Ascends: The Rise of a New Indian
     Elite - by Saurabh Mukherjea and Nandita Rajhansa for
     Marcellus Investment Managers in Apr 2023. https://
     marcellus.in/blogs/the-underdog-ascends-the-rise-of-a-
     new-indian-elite/
6   https://indianexpress.com/article/explained/explained-
     economics/explained-tamil-nadus-decentralised-
     industrialisation-model-9272702/

Epilogue: Back to Bengaluru to Witness the Dawn of a
New Era

1   https://data.worldbank.org/indicator/SE.ADT.LITR.
     ZS?locations=IN
2   https://www.statista.com/statistics/792074/india-
     internet-penetration-rate/
3   https://www.business-standard.com/article/
     international/english-gives-indians-edge-in-global-
     market-but-disparities-stark-report-122102300225_1.
     html
4   https://bhashini.gov.in/
5   https://sunbird.org/
6   https://peopleplus.ai/
7   https://ejaaduipitara.ncert.gov.in/
8   https://onest.network/

Scan QR code to access the
Penguin Random House India website